# It
# HAPPENED
# in
# HEAVEN

*Personal Stories of Inspiration*

# It HAPPENED in HEAVEN

## Personal Stories of Inspiration

*by*

**RABBI DOVID GOLDWASSER**

**FELDHEIM PUBLISHERS**

*Jerusalem / New York*

First published 1995

Hardcover edition: ISBN 0-87306-741-x
Paperback edition: ISBN 0-87306-747-9

Copyright © 1995 by
Dovid Goldwasser

FELDHEIM PUBLISHERS
200 Airport Executive Park
Nanuet, NY 10954

POB 35002 / Jerusalem, Israel


*Printed in Israel*

מכתב
מאת הגאון המפורסם
ר' אביגדור הכהן מיללער שליט"א

ב"ה

אדר א' תשנ"ה

כבר נתפרסם הרב דוד גאלדוואסער
כאיש הרוח להדריך בני אדם בדרך
התורה, ובחיבורו זה הולך לדרכו לעורר,
ולעודד, ולהרים קרן התורה, ויצליחהו ה'
שיפוצו דבריו בישראל.

נאום

אביגדור הכהן מילער

לעלוי נשמת

אבי מורי

ר׳ יצחק בן ר׳ ירוחם גאלדוואסער ז״ל

ולעלוי נשמת

אמי מורתי

מרת ריבא צערנא בת ר׳ בן ציון ע״ה

הכאב הולך וגדל,
במיוחד בשעות היפות בחיינו,
חולפת המחשבה
״לו היו עמנו עכשיו״

In honor of
our dear mother and grandmother
MRS. MIRIAM WEINBERG עמו״ש

and in loving memory of
our dear parents and grandparents
MR. YITZCHOK WEINBERG
ר׳ יצחק בן ר׳ אברהם שלמה ז״ל
and
ARON AND FEYGA KOYFMAN
ר׳ אהרן בן ר׳ ארי׳ לייב ז״ל
מ. פייגע בת ר׳ אשר זעליג ע״ה

*Leib and Linda Koyfman*

# Acknowledgments

## "Aromimcha Hashem Ki Dalisani"

THE VILNA GAON REMARKED that at each juncture of accomplishment in one's life, a *Yid* has to remember to thank Hashem for the *siyatta di-Shmaya* he was granted. *Shevach v'hodayah l'Hashem Yisbarach* for giving me the privilege to be *osek* in *avodas ha-kodesh* in my many different endeavors on behalf of the *klal.* It is through this work that I was *zocheh* to meet precious *nefashos*, some of whom grace the pages of this book. *Achas sha'alti me-es Hashem*— that I continue *ba-derech Yisrael sava* to be *marbeh k'vod Shamayim.*

I humbly express my *hakaras ha-tov* to the *ziknei rashei yeshivah* and *Admorim* who I have been privileged to be close to — too numerous to mention by name — and whose *hashpa'ah* on me is too vast to describe.

In appreciation of *Moran Ha-gaon* Reb Simcha Wasserman, *ztz"l,* whose awe-inspiring life is forever with me. *Daitan elecha.*

*L'havdil bein chayim l'chayim* to *Moran Ha-gaon* Rav Avigdor Miller *shlita,* whose *hashpa'ah* is felt wherever Jews are found. The Rav's inspiration and encouragement are ever present.

To my *rosh yeshivah, Ha-Rav Ha-gaon* Reb Chaim Leib HaLevi Epstein *shlita,* the *rosh yeshivah* of Yeshiva Zichron Melech.

To *Ha-Rav Ha-gaon* Reb Shmuel HaCohen Miller *shlita, rosh yeshivah* of Yeshiva Gedolah Bais Yisroel.

To the many Torah institutions that I have had the privilege of being involved with over the years, in particular the Agudas Yisrael of America, for their monumental work on behalf of the *klal.*

To R' Yaakov and R' Yitzchak Feldheim for their guidance and expertise. May they have continued *berachah v'hatzlachah* in all their efforts *lehagdil Torah v'lehe'aderah.*

To Leib and Linda Koyfman and their entire *mishpachah* for dedicating this volume. Leib and Linda are exemplary role models

9

for all to emulate. My close personal association with them over the years has been inspiring. Leib and Linda are paradigms of *chesed.* Their countless *chasadim* and *ma'asim tovim* serve as an inspiration to all who come into contact with them. May Hashem grant them *berachah v'hatzlachah, nachas, osher v'osher, arichas yamim v'shanim tovos.*

To Mrs. Nini Rubin, an unusually talented writer, whose brilliant editing of this work enabled me to precisely capture experiences and events I will forever cherish. Her wisdom and acumen infuse every project she undertakes with a special measure of blessing. May she, together with her family, merit *harbeh nachas, shefa berachah v'hatzlachah v'kol tuv.*

To Mrs. Simi Eichorn, whose *ibergegebenkeit* and selfless dedication know no bounds. For over a decade she has shared her talents, experience and organizational skills freely. Her wisdom, insight and keen observations have been the keys to success. *Kol ha-osek b'tzorchei tzibbur Ha-Kadosh Baruch Hu yeshalem secharam.* May she together with her wonderful family have *harbeh nachas shefa berachah v'hatzlachah.*

To the following people for their support and encouragement on this project. It is a privilege that I forever hold dear: Rabbi and Mrs. Mordechai Tzvi Abraham, Mr. and Mrs. Eddie Appelbaum, Dr. and Mrs. Leo Eisner, Mrs. Bertha Fox, Ari Goldstein, Rabbi Moshe Kolodny, Reb Sruly and Rochy Koval, Louis Leeder Esq., Rabbi and Mrs. Zechariah Lomnitz, and Rabbi and Mrs. Avram Ossey. There are additional names of *tayere chaverim* too numerous to list — *chaverim kol Yisrael.*

To Nachum Segal, a master of words and an eloquent spokesman for *klal Yisrael.* It is a privilege to have worked with Reb Nachum for over a decade. His unique talent and *kochos* have united *Yidden* from all walks of life. Our *kesher* and *yedidus* are immeasurable. May Reb Nachum together with his *aishes chayil* and family continue to have *berachah v'hatzlachah* in all that they do.

To my dear in-laws, Mr. and Mrs. Ben Koval, who carry on the royal lineage of the *chashuve* Kovalenko and Fink families: May they merit much *nachas* from their children, *einiklach* and *ur-einiklach, berachah v'hatzlachah, arichas yamim v'shanim tovos.*

I could never adequately express my *hakaras ha-tov* to my *aishes chayil*, Hinda Chaya. None of my work on behalf of the *klal* would be possible without her *mesiras nefesh*, unending patience, steadfast support and encouragement. The credit is to her. *Lo yichbeh balaylah nerah. B'ezras Hashem*, may we merit much *nachas* from our dear children, Yeruchem, Eliyahu Leibel, Fayga Chava and Hadassah. May they always go *b'derech she-hinchil lanu avoseinu ha-kedoshim* and may we merit to see *banim u-vnei vanim oskim ba-Torah u-v'mitzvos l'olmei ad*.

*Rosh Chodesh Elul*
Brooklyn, New York
*Ha-metzapeh l'yeshuah*
Dovid Goldwasser

11

# CONTENTS

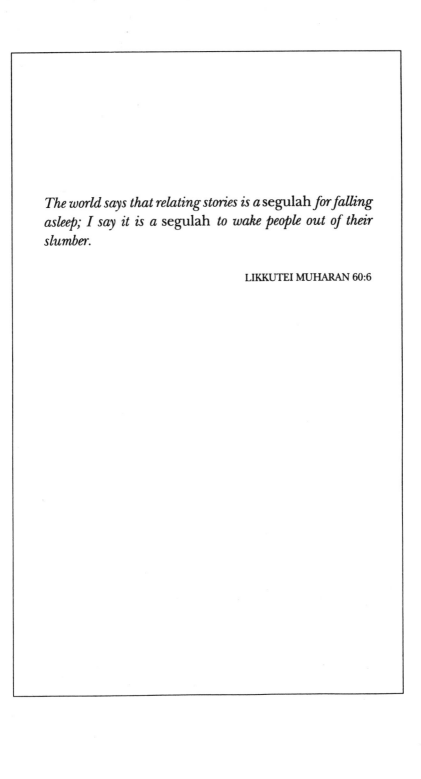

*The world says that relating stories is a* segulah *for falling asleep; I say it is a* segulah *to wake people out of their slumber.*

LIKKUTEI MUHARAN 60:6

# Introduction

TRAVELING DOWN AN UNFAMILIAR ROAD, a man notices a magnificent palace in flames. He looks around panic-stricken, expecting to see the owner, or better still, the fire brigade busily running with buckets of water. Only he sees no one. It appears as if the palace is abandoned. He wonders aloud, "Is it possible that a palace like this has no owner?" At that moment, the owner of the palace appears and declares, "I am the owner!"

Virtually the same thing happened to Avraham *Avinu* and attests to his greatness. He knew of the vast destruction brought upon both man and animal by the *Mabul* and the infighting and total dispersion of the *Dor Ha-pelagah*. This knowledge brought Avraham *Avinu* to declare, "Is it then possible that the world has no leader?"

Then the *Ribbono shel Olam* appeared to him and said, "I am the Creator of the world and there are Divine machinations behind everything that has happened in it since its creation."

We, unfortunately, are not on the spiritual level of Avraham *Avinu*. We cannot expect Hashem to reveal Himself and His ways to us personally. However, with a little acuity and a bit of perception we can see obvious manifestations of His hand in our daily lives. At times we are astonished; at other times we are perplexed. Yet, witnessing or even hearing stories about Hashem's *hashgachah* always inspires us...

Malkie and her parents came to see me in my office. "Rabbi, I need help. I have been going out now for five years, and I just can't seem to find the right one. I'll tell you the truth, Rabbi, I'm becoming discouraged and depressed about

16

it already. I just don't think I'll ever find my *zivug*. I go out, though it's not so often lately, and I already know before I even meet the guy that he's not for me. I know that it's all in Hashem's hands, but I wonder, when will I meet my *basherte?* Will I ever meet him? What should I do? What can I do? Rabbi, you've got to help me."

Malkie looked as if she were on the verge of tears, and her parents appeared emotionally drained, as if they'd had this conversation hundreds of times before.

I told them what they already knew — that Hashem selects a life's partner for everyone forty days before he or she is born. "His name was already called out in heaven as belonging to your name, Malkie. He's definitely out there. But Hashem decides when you will find him. There's a reason behind even the most inconsequential event and there is certainly some reason why you haven't become engaged yet."

As soon as I said these words, Malkie's face changed. This prompted me to ask, "Malkie, were you ever engaged?"

"No," she answered. However, she had paused a millisecond before replying.

Again I asked, "Malkie, *were* you ever engaged?"

This time, she just looked down at the floor without answering. I waited. Finally she said, "I was never *officially* engaged."

I asked her to explain.

"Well, you see, I never actually felt engaged. He was the one who thought we were engaged. We'd been going out for two months, and I liked him, but I just couldn't make that final commitment. I guess he misinterpreted how serious I was about our relationship. He thought we were unofficially engaged. Eventually, when I realized how serious he was, I broke it off completely. These things happen, Rabbi."

"Did you ever apologize for any hurt you may have caused this young man?" I asked.

She looked at me incredulously. "But, Rabbi! This happened several years ago. How could I possibly ask for *mechilah* now? He probably doesn't even remember me. He probably forgot the entire incident."

"Malkie," I suggested, "why don't you contact him and ask for *mechilah*?"

She looked at me incredulously. "But, Rabbi! This happened several years ago. How could I possibly ask for *mechilah* now? He probably doesn't even remember me. He's probably happily married and forgot the entire incident."

"Malkie, get in touch with him through a *shaliach* and ask for *mechilah*."

When Malkie's go-between contacted the young man, he said that he had been waiting all these years for her to apologize and had never forgiven her for the terrible pain she had caused him — until now.

Three months later Malkie called. She had become a *kallah*. Coincidence? Hardly. Everything that had transpired had already happened in Heaven...

# Preface

WHO DOESN'T LOVE a good story? To capture one's interest, to drive home a point, to illustrate someone's view of things, to teach a lesson, stories are a rich source of inspiration and guidance.

The great Chassidic master, Reb Elimelech of Lyzhansk, interpreted *"zecher rav-tuvcha yabi'u"* (*Tehillim* 145:7) to mean "a remembrance of Your abundant goodness will they utter" in a way that further amplifies this concept. Relating stories of the miracles and wonders Hashem has performed enables us to draw into the world even greater blessing than what was recounted. A fountain with a tiny hole can only release a thin trickle of water. Bore a few more holes in the spout, and a thin stream becomes a gush. Similarly, through retelling the abundant good Hashem has done, an immense upheaval is created in Heaven. The *ma'ayanos ha-yeshua*, the fountains of salvation, are opened and the world enjoys the supernal benevolence.

In the times of the *Beis Ha-mikdash*, we were obligated to travel to Yerushalayim three times a year — Sukkos, Pesach and Shavuos. No matter how far away a Jew lived, he would try to make the journey in order to bring the *korbanos*, the sacrificial offerings of the holiday. Interestingly, on the road to Yerushalayim there were no signs pointing the way. If a Jew wandered off the correct path, it was necessary for him to stop and ask for directions. This, according to our *meforshim*, was precisely the reason there were no signs. Wherever a traveler would inquire of his fellow, "Which way to Yerushalayim?" the fact that he was on his way to the *Beis Ha-mikdash* to be *oleh regel* became publicized. As a result, more and more Jews, who perhaps might not have made the effort, felt it incumbent upon themselves to join in the mitzvah and also set out for Yerushalayim.

There is also another explanation. Because there were no road signs to guide the traveler, of necessity, Jews had to connect and interact with other Jews in the course of their journey. Before they had to travel to Yerushalayim, Jews had never had much opportunity to meet anyone from a different city. They simply had no reason to leave their home towns. But things changed and three times a year Jews traveled and interacted with other Jews throughout the land.

Throughout my years in the *rabbanus*, I have traveled many roads in this long *galus*. Whether in Prague or Philadelphia, Moscow or Mississippi, Warsaw or West Virginia, I have encountered Jews of every stripe and persuasion: Sephardic, Lithuanian, Chassidic, Ashkenazic, *ba'alei chesed*, scholars, and Jews alienated from or completely ignorant of their roots. Along the way, I have been afforded the unique *zechus* of hearing, observing, and, at times, becoming part of the stories of their lives.

I was once asked to speak at a *Melaveh Malkah* fundraiser for a shul out on Long Island. As I was preparing a few remarks shortly before leaving, the telephone rang. Avraham, a young man I had known for many years, a dedicated *mechanech*, wanted to know if I could help him with his problem.

"My son, Shaye, is in a school for developmentally disabled children. *Baruch Hashem*, he's flourishing there. The teachers are specially trained for his disability, and he is actually beginning to learn the letters of the *alef-beis*. Every day, when he gets off the school bus, he is so proud of himself and his accomplishments. Only, we don't know what to do now. The school used to be funded by some very wealthy people, who, unfortunately, fell on hard times. The money they contributed has dried up, and now we were asked to pay seven thousand dollars a year tuition for Shaye. Rabbi, they want seven thousand dollars a year! On my salary that's a joke, only it's no joke.

"Shaye's only six, and he's so happy there! Could you give me any ideas? My wife and I are at the end of our rope. We don't know what to do. Our parents can't help us. Until now, we've always managed on our own, but this has just thrown us. If we can't come up with the money, we will have to enroll Shaye in the public school special ed program. There we won't have to pay, but what will be with his *alef-beis?*"

And then, to my sorrow, Avraham began to cry. It's not easy listening to a grown man cry.

I waited until he calmed down and then said, "Avrumie, don't worry. I will personally take it upon myself to raise the money for Shaye's tuition."

"No, Rabbi! I don't want to burden you with this. I was hoping you could maybe give me an idea of what to do. I guess I just wanted to talk to someone."

"Avrumie, please don't worry. I will see to it that you get the money for tuition." In between his protests, I managed to reassure him, though I didn't yet have the slightest idea where I could raise such a large sum.

Naturally, the plight of that heartbroken father and innocent little boy was very much on my mind when I spoke of the importance of *tzedakah* at the *Melaveh Malkah* dinner that night, and I related the contents of my recent phone conversation to my audience.

After I had finished speaking and was putting on my coat outside the coat room, a man in his mid-thirties, well-dressed and with a no-nonsense air about him, came over and asked matter-of-factly, "Rabbi Goldwasser, that little boy — how much is his tuition for the year?"

I replied, "Seven thousand dollars. But any amount is at

least a start."

"May I have your address?" After I gave it to him, the young man said *gut voch*, turned to leave, and then — again very businesslike — stopped and said, "Thank you for letting me know."

I was very moved by this expression of gratitude. I should have thanked him. Instead, he was thanking me for presenting him with the opportunity to fulfill a mitzvah.

Four days later, I received an envelope in the mail with an unfamiliar name on the return address. I opened it and inside was a check. I knew what the money was for by the amount written on it...seven thousand dollars.

A little boy's *neshamah* was saved in Brooklyn by a Jew on Long Island and I had the privilege of being the conduit of the Divine *hashgachah* that had brought their paths together...

One Shabbos summer afternoon in the Catskills, I was staying at a yeshiva camp. I was learning at a table right near the road, when a young man who was walking by stopped and asked for directions to a certain bungalow colony. After a short discussion, I realized that not only was the colony out of the *techum Shabbos*, but the young man had already walked well out of the *techum*. Since Jeff, as he had introduced himself, did not appear to be scrupulous about mitzvos, I could not decide for a moment whether I should inform him of this. After all, *techum Shabbos* is a complex part of *hilchos Shabbos*, and perhaps he would not understand or accept it. Then he would knowingly be violating the laws of Shabbos.

As we continued to speak, I sensed that Jeff was sincere and would probably be interested in hearing the facts, so I decided to tell him some pertinent details regarding the boundaries of walking distances on Shabbos.

Jeff's reaction was one of amazement. "I have never

22

heard of these laws and I would so appreciate it if you would take a few minutes to teach them to me."

I readily agreed and invited him to sit down at my table while I went to get the necessary *sefarim*.

Jeff was enthralled as we learned the various *halachos*. When we finished he said, "I am *shomer Shabbos*, Rabbi, so I guess I'll have to stay here the rest of the day."

It was *Shabbos Nachamu*, and the camp *rosh yeshivah* delivered an inspirational talk at *Seudah Shelishis*. I could see that the *rosh yeshivah*'s words, as well as the singing and general spirit of the campers, was having its effect on Jeff. After Shabbos, before he left for his original destination, he asked, "Do you think I could come by every now and then to continue our talks? This time, though, I'll come when I can drive," he laughed.

During the course of the summer, Jeff returned three times, and we learned and talked together. When the summer ended, I did not hear from Jeff, and after a while, the whole episode was forgotten.

Five years later, I was supervising a Shabbaton in Connecticut, and a group of leaders, young men in their twenties, were brought in to lead the learning groups and act as advisors throughout the weekend. One young man in particular caught my attention, as he was the most enthusiastic and successful of the group. Friday night, after the *seudah*, this young man came over to me and said, "Rabbi, do you remember me?"

I looked at him, but could not place him. "I'm sorry, you look a little familiar, but I don't recall..."

"That's okay, Rabbi. I guess it's hard to recognize me under this beard. But just to give you a little hint, I don't take any really long walks anymore — at least not on Shabbos."

I was momentarily bewildered, and then I recalled him. "Jeff," I exclaimed, "how are you doing?"

"*Baruch Hashem*, great. Since you saw me that summer I enrolled in a yeshiva in Israel, and I'm now in a yeshiva here. I guess you could say I've been learning ever since that first lesson you gave me on *techum Shabbos*. And do you know why? It was all because I stopped to ask for directions."

One thing I have learned during my years: We never know, as we travel along the path of life, where, when, or how we will make a difference — sometimes a small one, sometimes a monumental one. We only need to stop and ask directions...

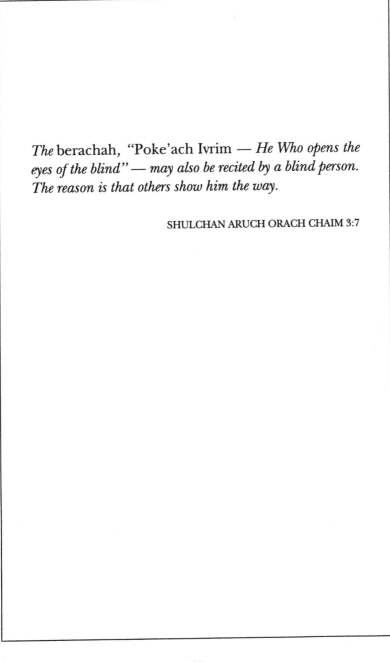

*The* berachah, "Poke'ach Ivrim — *He Who opens the eyes of the blind*" — *may also be recited by a blind person. The reason is that others show him the way.*

SHULCHAN ARUCH ORACH CHAIM 3:7

# *Sound Waves*

I was driving along the New Jersey Turnpike one early September afternoon on my way to a speaking engagement. As I drove, I thought back to the sequence of events that had led me to accept this very different sort of invitation.

Almost a year ago I had received a phone call from a representative of an international organization for which I had done some work in the past. He asked me to be the keynote speaker at their forthcoming convention, but when I checked my calendar, I found it overburdened, and regretfully, I was forced to decline.

Six months later, a delegation from this organization unexpectedly came to my home. They were determined to persuade me to change my mind.

"Rabbi," they said, "aside from how much it would mean to us, do you realize that you would be the first Orthodox rabbi to address our group? This would be your chance to reach out to a neglected segment of our People."

Sincerely and, ultimately, very convincingly, they advanced one persuasive argument after another, until finally I could no longer refuse. "It would be an honor for me to come and speak," I answered. Indeed, at the time I did not realize how unusual an experience this lecture would turn out to be.

Weeks later, as I stood at the entrance to the ballroom, the uniqueness of the event immediately impressed me. The room was crowded with hundreds of people. However, instead of the usual bursts of laughter amid the animated buzz of conversation that one would expect to hear when a group of this size gathers, there was an unceasing flurry of hand gestures and practically no intelligible sound in the room. I keenly felt that I had been afforded an awesome privilege to address this *olam*, despite the fact that they would not hear one word I said. Everyone attending this convention — man, woman, and child who had traveled to this little corner of New Jersey from practically every country in the world — was hearing-impaired and their only means of communication was through the continual motioning associated with sign language. This was the commonality that had brought these people together today. This and the fact that they were all Jews, though most were unaffiliated Jews.

As soon as I entered the room, I was surrounded. With the assistance of an interpreter or through guttural speech, I was earnestly asked *she'elos* that not many rabbis have to answer.

"Rabbi, what religious school in Eretz Yisrael do you recommend for my two deaf children?" asked one woman.

"Can a hearing rabbi perform a marriage ceremony for two hearing-impaired people?"

"I live in a small town in France where there are not many Jews, Rabbi, let alone hearing-impaired Jews. How will I ever find someone Jewish to marry?"

And on it went. Finally the organizers extricated me and I was led to the podium. I surveyed my audience from the stage. Rarely had I ever spoken before a group who appeared more eager to hear what I had to say. Yet, ironically, the only way they would be able to do so was through the interpreter at my side, who translated my words for them into sign language. I felt deeply touched and acutely emotional as I began to speak about the importance of performing even a single mitzvah in one's lifetime.

The moment I started, however, I could not help but notice that right in front, on the left side of the women's section, one middle-aged and one younger woman were creating quite a commotion. The younger woman, was gesticulating exaggeratedly and seemed to be rubbing the arm of the other one. I tried to ignore the disturbance so as not to ruin my concentration, but the more I tried to ignore it, the more my attention was drawn inexorably back to the pair. Occasionally, over the course of my years as a public speaker, I have had someone sit and knit while listening to me, but never did I have anyone in the audience who was so distracting. The exaggerated motioning did not stop, and I was fast approaching the point of becoming upset.

Why had they come to this session, I thought, if all they were going to do was disrupt it? How could I effectively communicate the importance of my subject matter if I was going to be persistently disturbed? Finally, exerting iron will and strong determination, I turned my head away and spoke to the rest of my audience, not glancing in their direction again. It was no easy task.

When I finished speaking, a line of people immediately formed to question me further about various issues that were of particular concern to the hearing-impaired community. I spoke to each person for a minute or two. Then, as the line shortened, to my utter dismay, I spied the two women who had so annoyed me. They were inching forward slowly and as they did, I saw with a start that the younger woman's hand was firmly grasping the elbow of the older woman to guide her.

Then I realized that the older woman's eyes were staring sightlessly ahead. They stepped up to me.

"Rabbi," the younger woman said, "my mother is blind and hearing-impaired, so she was unable to follow the interpreter. I had to sign what you said on her arm so she could *feel* the words. I wanted to ask you a question about one thing that you said. I want to be sure that I interpreted it correctly."

She told me what had confused her, and I assured her that she had indeed interpreted it correctly. Then I asked her to please tell her mother something for me.

As the daughter signed once again on the mother's arm, I said, "You may not hear and you may not see, but believe me when I tell you that your coming here today shows that you see what others cannot see and you hear what others cannot hear. May Hashem always be with you." The mother smiled and shook her head in acknowledgment.

As they turned away to leave, a television crew filming the convention rushed over to ask me to comment on the group's activities for their broadcast, but I was too overwhelmed to speak.

*Happy is the man who listens to Me, watching daily at My gates, waiting at the posts of My doors; for those who find Me find life.*

MISHLEI 8:34

The Be'er Avraham explains that when a person listens to Hashem, he doesn't just leave it at hearing, but he is also *shoked al dalsosai*— he goes into the *beis midrash* and the *beis knesses*. And once he is there, he clings to Hashem like the *mezuzos psachai*— in the same way that a mezuzah is attached to a doorpost.

# Master Key

THE RAV IS naturally at the top of the informal hierarchy that exists in a shul. He is the one who provides moral and spiritual guidance, who answers the *she'elos*, and who delivers the *derashos*. But there is another person in the shul whose efforts influence, if not in fact create, the close-knit feeling that exists among the shul members. He is the one whose *ma'asim* bring all the *mispallelim* together into a cohesive group. He is the person, everyone agrees, without whom the shul would not be the same. Sometimes his name is Reb Yaakov; sometimes it's Reb Shulim Mayer; and sometimes it's Reb Binyamin. But whatever his name, he is there in shuls the world over. He does not receive any material compensation for his work. Still, every morning before anyone else comes, he faithfully makes certain the door is open for early risers. He fills the samovar with water, and sets out the coffee, milk, and sugar. He neatly stacks the *siddurim*, the *Tehil-*

*lims* and the *Chumashim.* He collects money so the shul can buy an air conditioner or a sink. And amazingly, he remembers who has yahrzeit and needs to *daven* for the *amud.* He is not officially the *shammash* and neither is he really the *gabbai.* He is only a *poshute Yid* who loves the *beis midrash* and realizes the strong positive force it exerts over his fellow Jews' lives. Most importantly, he is someone who personifies the way a Jew ought to act. For what he does, he does not do for glory or *kavod* or remuneration. He is motivated solely by his love and concern for the well-being of another *Yid.*

 nce, on my way to a speaking engagement, I had occasion to *daven Minchah* in a *shtibel* in a small town. I was not in the shul for more than five minutes when a man in his late fifties came in. Tall and heavyset, with a warm and open countenance, he came rushing over as soon as he saw me, grabbed my hand, and excitedly began pumping it up and down.

"I know who you are," he exclaimed. "I remember you when you were a young boy. Your father *daven*ed in the same *shtibel* as my father. Do you remember my father, Reb Yaakov? I'm Izzy, his son."

The name triggered a memory of another solidly built man. I immediately exclaimed, "Of course I remember your father. Who did not know your father, and who did not cherish him? He was the pillar of the *beis midrash.*"

Then, to my listener's obvious delight, I recalled a few incidents about Reb Yaakov. I recounted how he was the one who always prepared something for the boys to eat right after *daven*ing in the morning, so they would not have to go off to yeshiva hungry. Izzy nodded vigorously and smiled broadly as I spoke. Who could forget Reb Yaakov? Every morning, without fail, in every kind of weather, he came to shul before anyone else, to unlock the doors and set up the room.

Izzy blinked away his tears as I spoke and then said, "It means a lot to me that you remember my father. I would like to tell you one final story about him.

"For thirty years my father was in charge of the keys to the *beis midrash*. Whatever else was happening in his life, he felt it was his sacred duty to be in shul by 5:30 every morning. I remember once my father came down with a very bad flu. He was coughing hard and felt really terrible. My mother begged him to ask someone else in the shul to open the door that morning. It was bitterly cold. She pleaded with him to stay home, but he refused, and sick as he was, he dragged himself to shul on time. Even when my father grew older and weaker and found it more difficult to walk, he never stopped coming to shul early and never gave up those keys to anyone.

"A short while after my mother died, my father became suddenly ill and had to be rushed to the hospital. I had been out of town on a business trip, and when I returned late that evening, my nephew called and told me. I rushed over to the hospital and found him lying in bed, looking deathly pale and barely able to talk.

"As soon as he saw me though, he called out in a weak voice that I could barely hear, 'Izzy, you're here. I was waiting for you.' Then he became agitated and tried lifting his head off the pillow. He motioned weakly with his hand and said, 'Izzy, the drawer. The drawer.'

"I said, 'Pop, please. Take it easy. Don't exert yourself. What's so important about the drawer?'

" 'Izzy,' he was really straining to speak now, 'Izzy, open the drawer. *Der shlissel, der shlissel.* Get it.'

"I couldn't help wondering: The key? The key to what? It must be the key to something important if my father was so concerned that I should have it. Could it be the key to a safety deposit box or some drawer where my father kept important papers?

"My father seemed to be using every last ounce of strength he had watching me anxiously to see if I had found the key yet. I opened the drawer quickly and took it out.

" 'Pop, I've got it,' I said reassuringly. 'I've got the key.'

"My father's head sank back onto his pillow. He looked relieved, but exhausted. By now he was barely able to talk. 'Izzy, I don't think I'll be able to come to shul tomorrow.' His voice was becoming fainter. I had to get very close to his lips to hear what he had to say. 'There are old people who come early. It's very cold outside. I don't want them to stand in the cold. Please, Izzy, make sure to be there to open the door. Take the key and be sure that the door of the shul is open on time. Make sure it's always open...'

"I stayed the rest of the night at my father's bedside. The key lay in my pocket, and I tell you, I felt like I was guarding a precious treasure. Believe me, I didn't take it lightly that my father had entrusted me with it.

"The next morning, my father's eyes flew open at 5:00 and very weakly he called to me, 'Izzy, it's time. Take the key. Go open the shul.'

"I was reluctant to leave, but my father kept insisting. Finally I went, since I saw he would not relax until I did. I got to shul at 5:30, just as my father had every morning for the last thirty years. I took out the key and unlocked the door. I prepared the coffee and the cups and stacked the *siddurim* neatly.

"While we were *daven*ing, the door of the shul was suddenly flung open, but it was not the ensuing blast of cold air that chilled me to the bone. In the doorway stood my nephew, and the look on his face told me everything.

"'Izzy,' he said, 'your father. They couldn't reach you.'

"Interestingly enough, we had just come to where the *Kaddish Yasom* is in the *daven*ing. Ever since that day, I have faithfully fulfilled my father's wishes. Every morning I open the shul door with the sacred key my father so valued."

*Epilogue:*

Years later I heard from a mutual acquaintance that Izzy remained the guardian of the shul for the next twenty years until the day he passed on to the next world. I also heard that the key to the *beis midrash* was buried beside him.

*The deeds of our fathers are a sign for the children.*

MIDRASH TANCHUMA, LECH LECHA 9

The Ramban comments, "It is for this reason that the Torah narrates at great length about the journey of the *Avos*, the digging of the wells, and other events...they all serve as a lesson for the future."

The roads our fathers walked during their lives provide us, their children, with the correct paths to travel during ours.

# Goldene Medinah

I met Seymour at a fundraising dinner. We were seated next to each other and he, in a very friendly manner, introduced himself. He was in his mid-fifties, tall and distinguished looking, every bit the image of the successful executive. As we talked, Seymour came across as warm, open, and eager to become better acquainted.

He was one of the top editors for a national magazine, had a wife, a son and a daughter and a huge house in Scarsdale. All the trappings of material success were in place.

"Spiritually, however, you could say I'm almost bankrupt, Rabbi. I've worked hard from the time I was sixteen. Those were different times. I never had the chance to go to yeshiva." He looked down and shrugged, "So this is how I turned out..."

I could see there was a lot more to Seymour than was obvious and said, "The fact that you are on the board of so many worthwhile institutions and contribute so generously to charity means you have learned important lessons about what being a Jew is all about, Seymour.''

"I appreciate your saying that, Rabbi, but to be honest, I know I should do better and more." Then Seymour's voice dropped as he confided, "There is one thing I am very strict about. One thing I have never been lax about in all my life." He stopped a moment, as if trying to decide whether he should continue. "I've never really told this to anyone..."

Then, amidst the clattering of dishes being removed and served, Seymour began.

"Although it was forty years ago, I remember it like yesterday. My mother and I left Poland by ourselves. My father had died the year before, and we decided to begin a new life in the *goldene medinah*, away from the hardships of the Old World.

"The accommodations on those ships were less than deluxe, and my mother and I booked passage in steerage. We were each allowed to take on board one package. I took some clothes, a few books — even then I would read anything. And my mother? Do you know what she took? Not her clothes, not her fine linens that were part of her trousseau — nothing but her pots and pans.

" 'Ma,' I asked her, 'what do you need those for? We can buy pots and pans when we get there.'

" 'No,' she insisted. 'I'm not sure we'll be able to buy kosher utensils there. Whatever a Jew eats affects him. I want to be sure we will always eat kosher. Leaving behind my pots and pans would be like leaving behind what we are.'

"I tried talking her out of it, but she was adamant. So there we were, lugging a very heavy package filled with my mother's cooking utensils on board the ship. And there we were, the laughingstock of the ship; the metal pots clanged and crashed into each other and all the other passengers turned around to look and jeer.

" 'Ha, what did you take those for? What do you think

you'll do with that junk? We're going to a new world. There's no place for these things from the Old World.' On and on they went.

"My mother remained silent. How embarrassed I was. How humiliated. I cringed at every derisive look thrown our way. I wanted to sink through the floor every time the ship heaved and those pots and pans clanged and clattered and everyone pointed and laughed.

"When the voyage ended and we were finally able to disembark, I felt relieved. But I deeply resented my mother's insistence on taking with us those loud announcements of what greenhorns we were.

"After clearing customs at Ellis Island, we followed everyone else and ended up in a cold-water flat above a store on the Lower East Side. But unlike the thousands of other immigrants, my mother simply couldn't acclimate herself to the New World. She couldn't face the squalor, the frenzied pace, the noise. She couldn't live with the loss of her world.

"Not long after we came here, it was about six months, my mother's broken heart just gave out and she passed away. I was in a daze of shock and grief. I didn't know how I would go on without her. We had been so close.

"After the funeral, I returned to the empty apartment. I went into the tiny, cramped kitchen to make myself something to eat. Bending down, I tried to take a saucepan out of the closet, but it was all the way in the back. I reached for it; in the process, the pots in front banged together. They made that sound once again and I was back on the ship, with everyone laughing at us. The embarrassment and shame I had felt flooded back for a second and then ebbed away forever. At that moment I felt how very much those pots and pans had meant to her.

"I knew then that I could never eat anything but kosher. I wanted to do that for her. Since that day, no matter where

I've been or with whom — and let me tell you, Rabbi, sometimes I have to eat with the biggest names in the industry at
the most exclusive restaurants — I keep the laws of *kashrus.*
It's my way of always remembering my mother.''

A publishing executive at a fundraising dinner — I had
only to open my eyes.

The Chasam Sofer explains that in the *pasuk* "*Sas anochi al imrasecha k'motzei shalal rav*" (*Tehillim* 119:162), the word *shalal* (spoils, treasure) according to *Chazal* refers to *bris milah*. What does this *pasuk* and the word *shalal* have to do with *bris milah*?

A person sometimes comes upon a treasure unexpectedly; he may even trip over it while traveling along a road. His reaction is one of great surprise. Here he found something of great worth by chance, and he didn't even have to work for it! Similarly, *bris milah* is this type of treasure; that is why it is referred to as a *shalal*. A Jewish male receives the *zechus* for fulfilling the mitzvah of *bris milah* and he did not even have to put forth any conscious effort to do so.

# *Birthright*

One never knows how much and in what way performing a mitzvah will recompense the person who participates in it with *sechar* in the World-to-Come and also immediate and unsurpassable gratification.

One night, at a wedding I was attending, Rabbi Shogalov, whom I knew from his work with Russian immigrants, approached me to ask if I would consent to act as the *sandak* at the *bris milah* of a four-year-old Russian boy. Of course, I agreed right away. Nevertheless, I confess there was a slight hint of reluctance in my acceptance. What would the *bris milah* of an older child, which necessitated a hospital, an operating room, and anesthesia be like? I wondered. Would not the antiseptic surroundings of the procedure completely negate its spiritual aspect? Despite my reservations, however, we agreed to meet at 7:00 the next morning at Interfaith Hospital in Bedford Stuyvesant.

Rabbi Shogalov was waiting in the hospital lobby when I arrived, and we greeted each other warmly. As befits a *Yiddishe simchah,* his demeanor and countenance were joyous. He led me to the waiting room, where I was introduced to Gregory, an eighteen-year-old boy, who was also to have his *bris* that morning, and Mr. and Mrs. Kushnir, the parents of Misha — "my" little boy, as I began to think of him.

I sat down next to Misha, an adorable blue-eyed blond-haired four-year-old, to become acquainted. I felt that the mood in that small, shabby hospital waiting room was nothing less than jubilant. Everyone seemed exhilarated and excited at the prospect of what was about to transpire. Misha and I talked together a bit and I was completely taken with his charming manner. His soft curls, which could not be contained by the regulation hospital cap, hung down to his eyes, and though he swung his feet — which did not reach the floor — back and forth in that slightly impatient manner children have, he did not fidget or fuss.

After a few minutes of friendly banter between us, a nurse came in with a wheelchair to transport him to the operating room. Obediently, Misha jumped off his chair to climb into it, but I quickly scooped him up in my arms and asked the nurse if I might carry him instead.

She hesitated a moment and then said, "Well, okay. Go ahead."

I held him tightly as I walked down the long hospital corridor, and although I felt my own heart beating hard with heightened emotion, he was relaxed and seemed completely unafraid. I placed Misha gently on the operating table. I had already changed into my hospital "blues," and everything was ready to begin. The anesthesiologist was hovering nearby. Misha looked up at me and asked in a small whisper, "Rebbi, what do I do now?" His eyes were large and trusting.

Gently I told him, "I think you must lie down now, Misha."

He lowered his little head very tentatively onto the pillow,

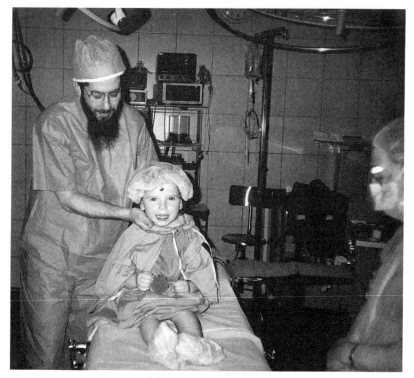

Misha on the day of his *bris.*

and then, just before the mask was placed over his face, Misha looked up, smiled broadly, and gave me a big wink. As the *bris* proceeded, I was very moved by the *mesiras nefesh* of this little boy, who was about to undergo something he did not fully understand, and yet he was so serenely accepting, only because he was told that this would make him a Jew in the truest sense.

The rituals of the *bris milah* were carried out, just as if it were a "regular" *bris.* But the fervor with which the surgeon, who was a *shomer Torah u-mitzvos,* and I made the requisite *berachos* and said the requisite passages, was as if supernal. I

44

left the operating room that day in a state of spiritual eupho-
ria, which floods back every time I remember... that wink.

Walking back to my car with Rabbi Shogalov after the *bris*,
he recounted some of the more unusual experiences he'd had
while working with the Russian community. The *hashgachah
pratis* (Divine Providence) of one incident in particular was
outstanding:

"One day I saw two young Russian men, who were walking along the street and talking," he began. "I am Russian, so
I approached them, introduced myself, and asked who they
were, where they were from, and what they were doing in the
U.S. The young men told me they were cousins from the city
of Dniepropetrovsk and had been able to secure temporary
visas to come to America, but that their families had to remain
behind. This was the Russian government's way of making
sure that their loyal citizens returned on time to the mother
country.

"Then I steered the conversation around to the question, 'Did either of you ever have a *bris milah*?' They seemed
a little startled by my asking, but answered no. When I asked
if they would be interested in having one, they declined right
away. I tried persuading them, explaining the significance and
holiness of the *bris milah*, but to no avail. Finally, I took their
names and telephone numbers — determined to try again
another time — and bid them good day. I was halfway down
the block when suddenly I heard someone running toward
me from behind. I turned around and saw it was one of the
young men I had just been speaking to.

"'Rabbi,' he called. I waited until he caught up with me.
'Rabbi, I don't care about a *bris* for myself. I'm too old. I'm
past it already.' I began to protest, but he interrupted, 'Rabbi,
listen. My wife just had a baby boy in the Soviet Union. You
don't think it would be possible for you to arrange a *bris* there
for *him*, do you?'

"Without a moment's hesitation, I answered, 'Certainly, we will make the arrangements immediately.' My *hashkafah* has always been that if a mitzvah comes to hand, one should take care of it without delay. But even as I spoke, it crossed my mind: How would I, a man standing on a street in Brooklyn, arrange a *bris* for a child thousands of miles away, in a country where *bris milah* was considered a criminal offense? It would take time and careful arranging, I thought, if it would be possible at all. Nevertheless, I suppressed my doubts and assured the young father I would do my best.

"As soon as we reached my office, I tried calling the *mohel* I knew in Russia. Now understand please, there was no direct-dial system and it was very difficult to reach someone there by telephone. But finally, after much dialing and redialing, I got the *mohel*'s wife on the line. She said, no, her husband was not home, and no, she did not know when he was expected. She sounded nervous to even be discussing her husband or his whereabouts over the telephone with me. I told her I would try again soon.

"The young man and I waited in my office. I felt very tense. I knew that to actually accomplish this task would require much *siyatta di-Shmaya*. After half an hour I called the *mohel* back. This time he was at home. I explained the situation to him, and after giving him the name and address of the family, he told me he could not make any promises, but he would try.

"I told him, 'The *ko'ach* of the mitzvah will help you succeed. You just try.' That was how it was left. He would try.

"The next day, the father of the baby called me. 'Rabbi, I want to thank you,' he said. 'I heard my little boy had his *bris* yesterday. We named him Zalman.'

"'Mazel tov!' I exclaimed. I was thrilled. 'May you have much *nachas* and may he grow up to be a credit to our People.'

"You can imagine my joy when the father added almost

offhandedly, 'Oh, by the way, Rabbi, isn't there something special about the eighth day and a *bris?* Did I tell you that yesterday Zalman was exactly eight days old?'

"I was overwhelmed. What a *zechus* to have been instrumental in this *Yiddishe neshamah* so far away having his *bris* on the eighth day, due to a chance meeting in the street. I have never forgotten that incident," concluded Rabbi Shogalov.

I thought of this remarkable story all the way home that day. I could only imagine the kind of reaction the baby's family must have had when suddenly a *mohel* appeared at their door out of nowhere to circumcise their child. I could also only imagine the extent of their *mesiras nefesh* — all of them, the mother, the grandparents, the *mohel* — for a *bris milah* was treated by the government as an illegal surgical procedure and was punishable by a lengthy prison sentence. It prompted me to remember the story of my own *zeide.*

*Zeide* had lived in Riga for most of his seventy-five years. Tall and erect, with a flowing, white beard and long frock coat, he was not only aristocratic in appearance, but was considered a member of the aristocracy of the town, even among the non-Jews. His well-bred and courteous ways, his scrupulous honesty and forthrightness, as well as his unwavering adherence to Torah and mitzvos made him revered and admired by everyone.

Even Mayor Gittis, mayor of the town of Riga, who was known to be a rabid anti-Semite, had developed a friendly, even close, but somewhat adversarial relationship with the *zeide.*

Over the past thirty years, they had spent much time discussing various issues that concerned the community. The *zeide* always suspected that Mayor Gittis actually enjoyed their intellectual jousting, though he pretended to become annoyed and angry at the *zeide's* convictions that quite naturally diverged sharply from his own. Nevertheless, Mayor Gittis continued his discussions with the *zeide* on a weekly basis.

Aside from his noble character — or, perhaps, because of it — the *zeide* had another claim to greatness. He had been the *mohel* in Riga for the past fifty years. For half a century, he had selflessly traveled hundreds of miles through many a bitter Russian winter in order to circumcise Jewish children.

Now, though, times had changed. The younger generation of Jews in Russia were greatly affected by the Communist suppression of religious practice. Their government-controlled education had led them to believe that practicing religious rituals only served to cause divisiveness within a "homogeneous" and "egalitarian" society of loyal citizens. They felt that it was necessary for their unity to eradicate any small residue of belief in anything other than the State. The punishment for being caught while *davening* in *tallis* and *tefillin*, or learning in a *Chumash*, or lighting a Chanukah menorah, had taken its toll on the present generation, with the result that many young people severed their ties, however tenuous, to their religion. And that included the mitzvah of *bris milah*.

In 1942, this tragic situation could not have been more pronounced. The *zeide*'s services were no longer in demand. Most of his family had already managed to leave Russia, but he had stayed behind. Now, however, at long last he had been able to secure an exit visa for himself. On the last evening before he was to leave, he was working in his study, sorting through papers and *sefarim* and packing whatever he felt he could safely take with him, when there was a knock on the door. He opened it. Standing outside was Pavel, a man, close to his own age, who had been a childhood friend. The *zeide* welcomed him in and the man immediately began to beseech him.

"My grandson is eight days old today. I want him to have a *bris milah*, and I know that tomorrow you will be gone. Please come with me now and circumcise him before you go," he begged.

Without a moment's hesitation, the *zeide* went back into his study, unlocked the special cabinet where his instruments were kept, packed them into an unobtrusive brown paper bag, put on his coat, and followed Pavel out the door. He knew that to perform a *bris milah* was a criminal offense, but this had never deterred him before and would not now, even on this — his last night in Russia.

The two men walked quickly along in the freezing cold. They realized that a certain amount of caution was in order, and spoke together in hushed tones, their feet crunching loudly on the firmly packed snow. Pavel kept looking behind them every now and then to be certain no one was following. As the two friends walked, they spoke of their almost forgotten days of youth, aware of the fact that this would probably be the last time they would see each other. The knowledge that on this last night they were performing a mitzvah was comforting.

When they arrived at the house, the *zeide* found the mother and grandmother anxiously awaiting his arrival. He wished them a hearty mazel tov and immediately began his preparations. As he was laying out his instruments and readying the infant, however, it occurred to him that he had not seen the father of the baby. Although he thought it a bit peculiar, he felt it would be ill-mannered to inquire about him and proceeded with great joy to perform the *bris*. In a few minutes it was over. The *zeide* and his friend pronounced the blessings, and the little boy became an authentic member of the Jewish nation.

After drinking a *l'chaim*, the *zeide* began packing up his equipment. Suddenly the door of the house was flung open, and the father of the baby stalked in. He took one look at the *zeide* and the instruments he was putting back in the bag, and his face turned red. He began screaming, "You had no right! You had no right! He's my son. I will report you to the authorities." He turned around and ran outside into the night.

Everyone stood frozen with shock and disbelief. Was he serious about his threat? the *zeide* wondered. Would he actually report a fellow Jew?

The *zeide* was concerned, but forcing himself to maintain a calm facade, he turned to the mother and began explaining how to care for the baby during the next few days. Then, after giving everyone *berachos* and saying mazel tov once again, he was about to leave, when once again the door was flung open. This time the father was accompanied by two hulking policemen. They grabbed the bag of instruments out of the *zeide*'s hand.

"What is this?" they demanded to know. The *zeide* just stood there, silent. He knew the evidence was incriminating. "You have surgical instruments here," they said as they emptied the bag onto the table, "and you have performed a surgical procedure outside of a hospital. You must come with us."

The mother and grandmother gasped and began crying as Pavel tried pleading with the police, but to no avail. The *zeide* was held roughly by the arms and led away.

After being arraigned in the courthouse the next morning, the *zeide* was forced to stay under house arrest, and, of course, his precious exit visa was immediately canceled. Over the next few months, a grueling trial was conducted, and the *zeide* was called to testify over and over, again and again. It began to seem as if he would remain mired in the Soviet mockery of a judicial system for the rest of his life, and he was beginning to despair of ever joining his family in America.

One fateful morning, the *zeide* was sitting in the defendant's chair, when he saw Mayor Gittis walk into the courtroom. What business did he have here? the *zeide* wondered. Why had he come? He watched as Mayor Gittis walked over to the judge and whispered a few words into his ear. The judge became agitated and answered in an excited manner, though his words were undecipherable. This went on for a few minutes. Mayor Gittis kept speaking to the judge in what seemed like an increasingly forceful manner, until finally — to the *zeide*'s astonishment — the judge, shaking his head angrily, banged his gavel on his table and announced loudly to everyone, "The case against Rabine Kovalenko is dismissed. The defendant is free to go."

The *zeide* could not believe his ears. After all these months, his ordeal was finally over. Moreover, it was a curious thing, but it seemed like Mayor Gittis had had something to do with securing his freedom. But when the *zeide* looked around for him, he had vanished.

Within the next two weeks, the *zeide* was miraculously able to secure a new exit visa, and once again it was the night before he was to leave Russia. Again he sat in his study, gathering together his belongings, and again there was a knock on the door. This time, however, one of the local peasants stood outside. "Rabbi, I have a message for you from Mayor Gittis. He asked that you meet him in the alley behind the community building on Gorkova Street at midnight."

The *zeide* was shocked and at a loss. Should he go? After all, he probably owed Mayor Gittis a debt of gratitude. But what if this was some kind of trap that would prevent him from leaving? In the end, the *zeide* decided to go. He had no other choice. If the mayor asked for the meeting, he must attend.

At exactly midnight, he arrived at the designated place. No one was there. The *zeide* felt uneasy as he stood waiting alone in the dark and deserted alley. After a minute, however, he saw Mayor Gittis approaching, walking briskly until they were face to face. He stood there for a moment, just looking at the *zeide*, not revealing anything by the expression on his face. Neither one said a word. They just looked at one another for what felt like a long time.

Mayor Gittis finally spoke. His voice was hard and cruel-sounding, and these are the exact words he said: "I had to tell you one thing before you go — before I never have a chance again. I hate you and despise everything you stand for." He paused for a fraction of a second, and then continued, "but I can't bear to see you go." Then Mayor Gittis broke down and wept as he walked away.

The next day, the *zeide* left Russia for America.

*Rabbi Yose ben Kisma said: I was once walking along the road when I met a man. He greeted me with, 'Shalom,' and I returned his greeting. He said to me, 'Rabbi, from what place are you?' I said, 'I come from a great city of scholars and sages.' He said to me, 'Rabbi, would you like to dwell with us in our place? I will give you a million gold dinars and precious stones and pearls.' I replied, 'Were you to give me all the silver and gold and precious stones and pearls in the world I would not live anywhere except in a place of Torah!'*

AVOS 6:9

The following question is asked: How did Rabbi Yose ben Kisma know that the place where he was invited to reside was not a place of Torah? He had never been there.

The Sefer Klei Chemdah answers that when Rabbi Yose realized that the topic of money was foremost in the man's conversation, he immediately understood the city was not a place of Torah. Thus, Rabbi Yose refused the offer to live there despite the fact that he would have been well-paid for it.

# The Silent Cry

Over the years, I have had the *zechus* of being Rav at Khal Bais Yitzchok in Brooklyn. I feel privileged to be the spiritual leader of such a *chashuve tzibbur*. The *daven*ing and the Torah learned in our shul have given me much personal satisfaction, and although I am the Rav and teacher, I confess that over the years of our association, I have learned much from my *mispallelim*. Their *achdus* and dedication to *chesed*, their warmth and love of Torah and mitzvos, all contribute to the special *ruach* that permeates our shul.

One of our very fine *balebatim* is Yaakov Spiegel. Yaakov is about thirty-five years old and lives near the shul with his wife and three children. He is a successful lawyer and a devoted husband and father. Often he brings his little boy, Daniel, to shul with him on Shabbos, and I am always impressed with the way little Daniel sits so patiently at his father's side, and how Yaakov always takes the time to point out the place in the *daven*ing to him.

One Monday morning the first year Yaakov began *daven-*

ing in our shul, he came over to me after *Shacharis* and asked which caterers we used, as he wished to give a *Kiddush* on the forthcoming Shabbos. I told him who would be acceptable, and then I asked him what the *Kiddush* was for. Instead of answering me directly, Yaakov said, "Rabbi, I'll tell you on Shabbos." My curiosity was aroused, but I did not question him further.

That Shabbos, I noticed that Yaakov was *daven*ing with an even greater than usual amount of *kavanah*. As soon as shul was over, we were asked to take a seat by the tables that had been set up earlier. Everyone heard *Kiddush* and ate something, and then the *gabbai* stood up, gave a little knock on the table, and introduced Yaakov.

"Thank you all for sharing in my *simchah* today," Yaakov began. "I would like to explain the reason for this *Kiddush* by telling you the story behind it. My wife and I have been celebrating this date every year for the past four years, going back to when we still lived in Connecticut.

"When Malkie and I were first married, we bought an old but beautifully refurbished farmhouse in Darien, Connecticut. We loved the place. It was a tremendous house with lots of room for the family we planned to have. The grounds around the house were spacious. In the backyard there was a huge old oak tree, whose massive branches brushed against the upper-story windows, and there was a large wooden front porch where we could sit in the nice weather. It was a place we'd always dreamed of.

"To be honest, though, there were some drawbacks. For one thing, I had a long commute to my job in the city by train. The traveling was tiring, but we felt it was worth it in order to enjoy the serenity of suburban living. Another disadvantage, and one we couldn't overlook that easily, was that there were not very many Jews in Darien. There were some, but they didn't live nearby. The nearest Orthodox shul was a good mile-and-a-half down a quaint little country road that had no lights and a very rudimentary amount of paving. Walking to and from shul on a Friday night required the sure-footedness of a tightrope walker and built-in radar besides. Then, of course, once we had a family, with the grace of Hashem, although we had loads of room for our kids to run and play, who would be their playmates? Well, we consoled ourselves, you can't have everything. We'll worry about that when the time comes. In the meantime, we were content. Maybe a little lonely — there was no *shiur* to go to at night, and there wasn't really anyone to send *shalach manos* to, and nobody nearby to say "*gut Shabbos*" to — but it was a small price to pay, we told ourselves again and again.

"After a year, *baruch Hashem,* we had a little boy. Naturally, every first-time parent is ecstatic and we were no different. The joy of our first child was a joy that simply towered over everything else that had ever happened to us. It was the most precious gift we could ever have imagined from Hashem, and Malkie and I certainly appreciated its magnitude. But his *shalom zachar* was a quiet one — it couldn't be helped. Also, there wasn't a *mohel* in Darien — we had to import one from New York. And there were no children to say *Shema* by the baby's crib the night before his *bris*. Nevertheless, it was a tremendous *simchah,* and we named our little boy Daniel.

"Little Daniel had everything a baby could need or want. Malkie had redecorated his room with brand new wallpaper covered with cute little pictures of all kinds of farm animals. There were newly-installed windows (we didn't want the room to be drafty), and we had the nicest crib, infant seat, and changing table that could be bought. We decided not to worry now about where Daniel would go to yeshiva, or what kind of friends he would make in Darien, or how he would be able to walk with me so far to shul.

"Our routine was such a pleasant one. We were so

content. These nagging thoughts were on the back burner, and we dared not even discuss them. After all, we had everything: the perfect house, the perfect baby, the perfect life.

"Then, one frosty night in December, when Daniel was eight months old, on what started out as an ordinary evening, everything changed. The day had been uneventful. Malkie had been busy with her usual routine. I had come and gone from work, and after dinner we were sitting on the couch by the fireplace, talking about our respective days as Daniel played happily with one of his many toys. He had been acting fine all day and when Malkie picked him up to ready him for bed, he smiled and gurgled.

"Like model first-time parents, we had read all the parenting manuals available in the English language and we knew how important a bedtime routine was. So we made sure every night to follow the same pattern. At exactly 7:00 Malkie or I would bathe Daniel, dress him in his pajamas, take him over to kiss the mezuzah, give him his bottle in the crib, and then say *Shema* while he listened. After a good-night kiss, we'd close the door and it worked like a charm. He'd go right to sleep and stay asleep right through the night.

"That night the routine went smoothly, as usual. However, as soon as Malkie put Daniel into his crib, he began crying hysterically. Malkie was surprised. She picked Daniel up, held him until he quieted down, and then tried putting him back in. He cried again, even more loudly and even more hysterically. Malkie couldn't understand it. She held Daniel in her arms and soothed him. He quieted down and seemed content. She felt his forehead; it was cool. He seemed fine. But no matter how she or I tried to put him back in his crib, each time Daniel began to cry pitifully.

"We decided to put Daniel to sleep in our room. Sure enough, with a few gentle pats, he went right to sleep. When we were sure he was fast asleep, I picked him up very gently and tiptoed quietly down the hall with him to his room. No sooner did I put him back in his crib than the same thing happened again: loud, choking sobs. This went on all night. When we brought Daniel to our room, he would fall asleep. When we tried putting him in his crib, he started crying.

Finally, near daybreak, I decided that the situation was out of hand. Obviously, there was nothing physically wrong with Daniel since he slept peacefully in our room. So I said to my wife, 'There is nothing wrong with this child. He's probably just getting spoiled. Didn't we read that you sometimes have to let a baby cry himself to sleep for his own good? Put him back into his crib and just let him cry. He'll eventually fall asleep.'

My wife reluctantly, carried the baby back to his room and put him in his crib. This time, however, Daniel didn't cry. He just lay in his crib, with his eyes wide open, staring at the ceiling. Malkie walked out of his room and closed the door. Daniel didn't make a sound.

"When she came back to our bedroom, Malkie told me how strange it was the way Daniel was just lying there, with his eyes wide open. I could see she was very uneasy as she finally lay down to sleep.

"Suddenly she jumped up, and exclaimed, 'I'm bringing the baby back here.' For some reason, she did not walk. She ran down the hall to Daniel's room, flung open the door, and grabbed him out of the crib. She held him tightly as she carried him quickly back to our room.

"The moment she crossed the threshold, we heard a loud crash. We ran into the hall to find out where the sound had come from. It had come from Daniel's room. Flinging open the door, we were horrified. The entire ceiling had fallen down and every piece of furniture in the room was smashed to pieces — including Daniel's crib.

"Our gratitude to Hashem for saving Daniel was boundless. Not long after, we sold the farmhouse and moved to a Torah community in Flatbush. True, we miss the porch and the fireplace and the large backyard sometimes, but we know that we have found something even more valuable: a place where our children can go to yeshiva and make proper friends, a place where they can see Torah being learned and *chesed* being done, a place where mitzvos are performed. In short, we've come to a place where children can grow up in an atmosphere that will be conducive to their becoming *bnei Torah* and *yirei shamayim*. It's really not much of a trade-off.''

*Ben Bag-Bag says: Concerning the Torah it says turn it over and go through it, for everything is in it.*

AVOS 5:26

The Kotzker Rebbe says that only through the Torah can we turn ourselves around.

# Daily Bread

When Mr. and Mrs. Adams phoned me at my office one morning, they were vague about the nature of the problem that had prompted them to ask me to help their eighteen-year-old daughter. However, they wanted to arrange a meeting for as soon as possible.

A wealthy, upper-crust family from Connecticut, the Adamses sounded extremely refined over the phone. So when my secretary came into my office to announce their arrival, I could not understand why she appeared so shaken. Very quickly, however, I understood when I met their daughter.

Alicia came into my office holding her mother's hand tightly. The only way I can describe the way she looked is to say that her face was as white as freshly-fallen snow, and like snow, flakes of her skin were falling onto her shoulders. It was horrific to see a teenager looking so grotesque. Obviously Alicia was quite ill, but I did not yet know what the nature of her illness was. She sat down and requested that her mother wait outside. She said she would like to tell me her story, but asked that I keep it confidential.

"You see, Rabbi," she began in a soft, dreamlike voice, "I am trying to become truly pure. I see that fulfilling one's physical needs only leads a person to activities and pursuits that are not conducive to spirituality. I want to cleanse myself so that I will become worthy of reaching a high spiritual level. I feel that I must reach my Divine purpose in life, Rabbi. Every human being must answer to his higher calling. I believe we were put here on earth to accomplish spiritual things, not to gratify our physical desires."

I asked her, "Alicia, how do you go about achieving this purity?" fearful of the answer I would receive.

"Well," she answered, "I try not to eat too much. I want to limit the physical sustenance that enters my being so that it will not cause me to become impure."

Then I understood what was causing Alicia's wraithlike and sickly appearance. She was anorexic, and from the way she looked, it had already taken a horrible toll on her health. She looked like she had come to the end of her physical stamina and it would not be much longer before her strength and the last remnant of her health would be depleted. Now I understood the urgency in her parents' request to see me. Alicia was starving herself to death.

I knew that urging her to eat or trying to show her that she was slowly committing suicide would be futile. I remembered reading about how one anorexic cut a raisin in half, ate half the raisin for dinner and thought she had overeaten. Without the nutrition she needed, her body would come to fail her. I wanted to help this young *neshamah*, but I knew it would be very difficult. I quickly rose from my desk and strode over to my bookcase. I took down a large volume of Talmud, *Bava Metzia*, and made a show of opening it.

"Alicia, I want to help you in your quest for spirituality. I have here a volume of the holy Talmud." I showed her the page I had turned to.

"It says here that in order for a person to derive genuine spiritual benefits that will sustain him throughout the day, he must eat *pas shacharis* — morning bread. This gives a person the spirituality he needs to carry on his activities for the rest of the day."

Alicia looked a little surprised. "Does this mean for everybody?" she asked.

"Yes, Alicia," I answered, "it means for everybody...even for you."

She seemed intrigued and asked, "How much am I supposed to eat?"

I told her, "In order to recite *Ha-motzi*, you should eat one whole slice, but no more than that. On Shabbos, however," I added, "you must eat two slices, one in the morning and one in the afternoon." I told her the minimum because I knew that if I said to eat more she would immediately stop listening to anything I said.

Alicia nodded thoughtfully and seemed to ponder my instructions. I had no idea whether she would obey them, or even if, at this point in her debilitated condition, she would be able to.

After she walked out of my office, still deep in contemplation, her mother came rushing in and asked what had happened. I gently explained that I had spoken to her daughter in confidence and could not at this point divulge what had been discussed, but I asked Mrs. Adams to let me know what transpired at home. I could only hope that my advice would have a good effect on Alicia.

A few days later, Mrs. Adams called me. "Rabbi!" She sounded as if she were barely able to suppress her joy. "The strangest thing happened the morning after Alicia spoke to you. I was in the kitchen, drinking a cup of coffee, when suddenly she came in. I was very startled. After all, Alicia has not been frequenting the kitchen much in the last few months. Then," she continued, "she went over to the bread box and took out a slice of bread. She washed her hands, took the bread into the other room, and ate it in privacy. Rabbi, a whole slice of bread!" Mrs. Adams sounded exultant. I was very happy to hear this, and I asked her to keep me up to date on what I had *bitachon* would now be Alicia's continued progress on the road back to complete good health.

Mrs. Adams called me a week later to inform me that now, aside from the bread Alicia was eating regularly, she had noticed her eating other things during the day. Obviously, the old *Yiddish* proverb, "*Fun essen kumt appetit* — one's appetite increases as one begins to eat," was true.

Every kind of wisdom and knowledge is contained within the lines of our holy Torah. One need only search to find the answer, or in Alicia's case, the *refuah*.

*Epilogue*:

The breakthrough for Alicia came by means of the Torah. However, this did not preclude her receiving extensive, competent psychological assistance in order to attain a complete recovery.

*If I wanted to, I could bring the dead back to life. But my purpose is to give life to the living.*

R' MENACHEM MENDEL OF KOTZK

# *Wake Up Call*

There is always the question of whether to leave the phone on full volume or to lower it before retiring. After all, no one relishes being awakened in the middle of the night. In our house, however, the decision is usually made to keep it plugged in "just in case." Thus, it was at 3:00 A.M. when I was jarred awake by the shrill sound of the phone ringing. I grabbed it after one ring.

"Hello, is this Rabbi David Goldwasser?" The voice on the other end of the line was not only unfamiliar, but had a gruff edge to it.

"Yes, this is he."

Then in a very businesslike manner, "Rabbi, I'm Officer Costanza of the N.Y.P.D. I've got a young lady here who is standing on the roof of her apartment building, ready to jump. She says you're her rabbi, so maybe you could talk to her. She's serious , Rabbi. She won't let us come within two feet of her, and she looks like the real thing. She just wants to speak to you first. Her name is Elaine Smith."

66

I had never received a phone call like this before. From the midst of a deep sleep I had been thrust into the middle of a life and death situation that required the sharpest mind, the most persuasive tongue, and the greatest *siyatta di-Shmaya*. I could only pray that all three would materialize in time. I did not recognize the young lady's name, but before I even had a chance to answer, I heard him hand the phone to Elaine.

She at once began to speak in a slow and steady monotone. "I can't go on anymore. I just want to end it all. The difficulties I've been having...they're just too much to bear. I can't take it any longer. I just want it to end. The pain I'm in... Going to school didn't help. My existence — it's too painful. I'm alone. Don't you see that? I've tried to help myself, but I just can't seem to do it. I just can't. Nobody understands me. I want to put an end to this misery..."

Elaine continued her diatribe for what seemed like a very long time. As she spoke, I paced back and forth with the phone pressed hard against my ear, alternately sweating and shivering. A human life hung in the balance. I trembled at the knowledge that such a dejected *neshamah* needed a reason to continue and that I had to supply her with that reason. Ironically, the only thing that stood between Elaine and a horrible death thirty stories below was the instrument of communication that she and I held in our hands.

She paused for a second. Quickly, before she could start again, I said, "Elaine, don't ever give up. A Jew doesn't give up. Our Rabbis said that as long as a person lives there is hope. You have not exhausted every possibility of hope. You are young and you have many years ahead of you — happy years, fruitful years. Don't let this moment of desperation cloud everything you've accomplished in your life so far..."

She charged in loudly and with bitterness, "That's not true! I haven't accomplished anything. I'm not a good person. I don't deserve to live." Then quietly with a stifled sob, "Help me! I'm in pain."

I could tell from her voice that Elaine was becoming more dejected by the minute. My mind raced. What could I say? How could I veer her thoughts away from this demoralizing trend? Suddenly it came to me. I had met her once at a symposium for Jewish professionals in upper Manhattan, where I had delivered a lecture about four years ago. I remembered a mention of parents, so I quickly asked in as casual a way as possible, "Elaine, how are your parents?"

To my complete horror, she began yelling, "Why do you ask me about my parents? What do they have to do with this? Why did you mention them?" She kept on and on while I futilely tried to calm her down.

"Elaine, I only wanted to ask how your family was doing. Your parents have nothing to do with this. You're absolutely right. I only..."

Abruptly, she interrupted me. "Why aren't you here?"

"Give me fifteen minutes and I'll be there," I answered quickly.

Again she started screaming, "No! Don't go. Don't hang up. Don't get off this phone." Then she began rambling along in the same vein: She was worthless. She wanted to end it all. No one understood her. Then, "Why aren't you here?"

I repeated my offer to jump into a cab and be there in fifteen minutes.

Then she announced, "That's it! I'm going to end it. I've had enough of this talk." She sounded completely sincere. Desperately, I wondered what I should say. Should I take a chance on reminding her about how she would be hurting her parents? No. Obviously that was a sensitive subject. Should I quote *Chazal* about the sacred value of a human life? My mind was a miasma of thoughts and questions.

I forced myself to retain at least a veneer of calmness. "Elaine, I accept your decision. But I still have one question

I would like to ask you. What shall I tell your *chasan?*" Suddenly she became still. There was absolute silence for a second. Then Elaine answered, in a subdued voice, "I don't have a *chasan.*"

"That's not true!" I countered. "Forty days before a baby is formed, a Heavenly voice proclaims: The daughter of this person will marry that person. Every *Yiddishe neshamah* that comes to this world has a *zivug* somewhere. So that means that there is a *chasan* somewhere waiting for you, too. And I just want to know what to tell him in case he asks me about you."

"You mean even I might one day stand under a *chuppah?*"

"Elaine, I honestly believe so."

The next thing I heard over the phone was bitter crying and a great deal of shuffling sounds. Then the original gruff voice came back on the line, only this time there was an undercurrent of strong emotion. "Okay, Rabbi, we've got her. She's fine. We've got her. You did a good job, Rabbi, and God bless you."

I felt drained and euphoric at the same time. I had already been blessed by Hashem. He had given me the *da'as* to use the appropriate words and reasoning.

R' Nachman of Breslov has a most interesting *sichah* on *shidduchim* and *zivugim*.

R' Nachman says that there are many *shidduchim* on various levels. In some, the possibilities of the match are discussed by third parties. In other cases, the young man and young lady actually meet and in other instances, they may continue to see each other. Some *shidduchim* progress even further — to the stage of engagement and marriage, when the *shidduch* becomes a *zivug*.

# Shidduchim and Zivugim

From all appearances, Shlomo was a confirmed bachelor. He was forty-two years old, very presentable looking, financially secure, and never married. Nonetheless, if the word ''confirmed'' connotes a determination to remain single, it did not apply to Shlomo. On the contrary, he was extremely anxious to find his *zivug* and begin building a Jewish home. For years, friends, acquaintances, and business associates had someone ''just perfect'' for him to meet. Unfortunately, their idea of perfection was never in sync with Shlomo's. From time to time, when I would speak to him, he would confide that he was lonely and was beginning to despair of ever meeting the right one. After all, he had been searching for twenty years with no success.

Then, one fine September morning, Shlomo called to relate the good news that he had become engaged. I was very happy for him and wished him mazel tov. He asked to come over with his *kallah*, and then added — somewhat mysteriously

— that there was an amazing story behind their engagement which he was anxious to tell me. When Shlomo arrived with his *kallah*, Rochel, I could see that a strong *kesher* had already formed between them and they both appeared elated at the prospect of their forthcoming marriage. We drank a *l'chaim*, I extended my wishes that they have a long and happy life together, and then I saw that Shlomo was simply bursting to get on with his story.

"Rochel had been married before," Shlomo began, "and she had kept her former husband's last name. She had an apartment on the West Side and, naturally, when we dated, I picked her up there.

"When things became serious, she asked me to come to Brooklyn to meet her parents. Of course, I agreed immediately. Even at my age, I was still a little nervous at the prospect of meeting my future in-laws. I hoped they would approve of me and that we would get along well. So when we stood at the front door of her parents' apartment, I wasn't thinking about anything but making a good impression.

I glanced casually at the name on the bell and it occurred to me that until that moment, I had not bothered to ask Rochel what her maiden name had been. For some reason, the name on the bell was very familiar, but I couldn't remember why.

"While I was being introduced to my future father-in-law and as we spoke a few words together, I saw that he kept glancing curiously at me, as if he knew me from somewhere, and for some reason I kept wondering the same thing. I was so distracted. I just couldn't stop wondering about where I had seen their name before. It was like a tune going around in my head whose name I just couldn't remember.

"Rochel's father inquired about my family, where I was from, what I did for a living — the usual things a father is interested in when his daughter brings home her *chasan*. I answered politely, but my distracted expression bothered my future father-in-law and finally he asked me point-blank, 'Shlomo, what's the matter?'

"So I told him what was on my mind. I asked him if maybe we had some friends in common or maybe some distant relatives. No, he didn't know any of my friends or relatives. I asked him what line of work he was in. He told me he had a furniture business. That was it! I realized immediately where I knew the name from. Twenty years ago, when I had rented my first apartment, I had bought my furniture at his store.

"Rochel and her mother were amazed at the coincidence. I was originally from Queens and my apartment was in Manhattan. I rarely went to Brooklyn. And of all the hundreds of furniture stores in all three boroughs, I had ended up buying my furniture from this particular store!

"The truth was that I had been in Brooklyn that day on business, right in the neighborhood. I hate to shop. I knew I was moving into my apartment the following week and still had not furnished it. So when I saw the store right there, I just walked in off the street and bought everything I needed in ten minutes. Until this very moment, I had completely forgotten about the incident.

"Then my father-in-law said, 'Put your coat on, I want you to come with me.' It was a freezing cold night, and I did not particularly relish the idea of going out for a mystery trip. But I was not about to refuse my *kallah*'s father's request, and dutifully I put on my hat, coat, and scarf and followed him out the door. I kept wondering, where are we going?

"We parked in front of his furniture store. He unlocked the gates and then the front door. He took me down into the basement and began sifting through boxes and boxes of records and papers. After about ten minutes, he cried out excitedly, 'Here it is! I found it!' With a beaming face, he handed me an invoice and proclaimed, 'Just as I thought; just as I thought.'

"I could not imagine what was so remarkable about an invoice that excited him to such an extent. He handed me the slightly yellowed piece of paper. 'Look at it,' he said, triumphantly. 'Look at it carefully.'

"I examined the invoice word by word, lest I miss something important. Surprisingly, my name was on top. Then my old address and telephone number. Then a list of the items I had bought: one couch, two upholstered chairs, and a dinette set. I looked up from the paper at my father-in-law. I was a little baffled.

"He was standing there smiling expectantly and nodding his head encouragingly. 'Keep going,' he urged.

"On the bottom was the promised date of delivery. I recalled there had been some problem with the delivery, and that I had called and spoken a few times to the person who had taken care of me in the store...and there on the bottom of the invoice was the signature of that person — my *kallah*!

"Rabbi," he concluded, "Twenty years ago the *shidduch* was made, and it took twenty years until the *shidduch* became a *zivug*."

*To tell a story, one needs to be skilled. But what requires even more skill is to know how to listen to one.*

REB SHOLOM DOV BER, THE RASHAB

# All in the Mind

When I moved to New York City, one of my first positions was with a national organization whose offices were in midtown Manhattan. My responsibilities were varied and interesting and in the course of my work, I was privileged to come into contact with many fine and distinguished individuals — *rabbonim*, lay leaders, community activists, businessmen — a cross section of the Jewish community.

But it was on one seemingly average afternoon that I encountered a person so remarkable that I can still vividly recall our first meeting. One of my work colleagues had been urging me for months to eat lunch with him at a popular *milchig* restaurant near our office. I had always declined as it is not my habit to eat in restaurants, but somehow this particular afternoon I felt I could no longer do so without insulting my friend. So around noon I found myself walking with him the three blocks over to the restaurant. As we walked, we became engrossed in the discussion of an important issue that had come up during the day.

A middle-aged waitress greeted us as we entered the restaurant and showed us to a table. Our conversation continued as she covered the table with a clean, white cloth. Then, suddenly and quite amazingly, the waitress broke in and began quoting some *Rishonim* and *Acharonim*. This continued without pause as she placed our water glasses, silverware, and menus on the table.

I was astounded and stopped mid-sentence to look up. The woman appeared to be in her late fifties. Outwardly, she was probably just like ten thousand other food servers in New York City. Inwardly, however, this woman was very different. From what she was saying, it was obvious she was learned. In fact, she was quoting chapter and verse from the most diverse *mefarshim*.

She placed the bread basket and condiments on the table, and then waited with her pencil poised over her pad, ready to take our orders. She had stopped speaking.

Quite honestly, I was awestruck. I looked at my friend, but he was studying the menu quite nonchalantly.

After she took our orders and went back to the kitchen, I asked, "Who is that waitress? Where does she come from? How does she know all that?" I could barely contain my amazement.

My friend, however, just shrugged offhandedly. "Oh yes, I have heard her quote before. Come to think of it, she does know a lot."

My mind was filled with questions. Where did this woman learn Torah in such depth? Why was she a waitress when she had such a rich Torah background? I was sure she would have a fascinating story to tell, but I did not feel comfortable asking her all sorts of personal questions. Therefore, when it was time for us to return to the office, I left without any answers.

This incident continued to gnaw at me for weeks, but I

was ambivalent about returning to the restaurant, and probably never would have, had not Mr. Plony, a well-known philanthropist and one of our organization's largest contributors, not come to pay us a surprise visit one afternoon.

My colleague was out to lunch, and since I knew he had been trying to contact this individual, I grabbed my overcoat and ran down to the restaurant to fetch him. As soon as I opened the door, the waitress came rushing over and said to me in Yiddish, *"Ich bet mechilah* — I beg your forgiveness. I hope I didn't offend or insult you. I know it's not your way for women to join in Talmudic discussions..." She continued apologizing. There were tears of remorse in her eyes. "I hope you will forgive me. If that's why you've never come back to eat here, I promise I will never bother you again..."

I stopped her. "Please, there is absolutely no need to apologize. On the contrary, I was inspired by your enthusiasm and interest in the *divrei Elokim chayim.* In fact, I wanted to hear about where you acquired your remarkable knowledge."

Upon hearing this, her face, which had been furrowed with lines of contrition a moment earlier, relaxed into a happy and proud smile. "Won't you please have a seat so I can serve you something?" she asked eagerly.

I looked around the restaurant. I saw that my colleague was no longer there and assumed we had probably missed each other on the way over. I answered, "Only a cup of tea."

The waitress bustled quickly into the kitchen and came back a few seconds later with a fresh, warm piece of *mohn* cake and my cup of tea. It didn't take more than a moment before Chava — as she had introduced herself — proceeded to quote a fascinating Magen Avraham on *hilchos Shabbos* and then bring in a question from the Pnei Yehoshua as well as a complex Rambam on the same point. Chava could undoubtedly pass muster in the finest yeshiva.

When she was finished speaking, I asked her, "Chava, tell

me your story. How is it that you know so much? You realize that it's not usual for a waitress to be as learned as you."

"Thank you," she answered, "but I wish I could learn more. Sixty years ago I was born in Czechoslovakia. The *Ribbono shel Olam* blessed me with a quick mind, but I was a girl. And you know, Rabbi, in those days girls didn't learn much more than how to *daven* in a *siddur*, and some not even that. My father, may his memory be blessed, was a very wealthy and influential businessman, but also a big *talmid chacham.* Whenever any *rebbes* or *roshei yeshivah* of the time would pass through our town, they would stay at our house for a day or two. Of course, my father would always give them a generous donation. But he would also spend hours locked in the study, learning with his revered guests.

"I was an only child and always very interested in learning. But as a girl, I never dreamed of entering the study and being privy to my father's discussions. What I did, though, was to stand outside my father's study door and listen. I would stand motionless there for hours, with my ear pressed against the thick wooden door, and I would listen as though my life depended upon it. Afterwards, I would look through my father's bookcases for all the *sefarim* he had mentioned, take them down and study them myself, trying to piece together what I had heard. I spent hours doing this until I guess you could say I became knowledgeable, although I had never had much formal schooling."

"Then the war broke out. My father lost everything: the house, his business, his family, everything. And I? I lost my father and an entire way of life. What we went through..." She paused a moment, staring at the floor, obviously lost in painful remembrance. "I too lost everything — things that can never be replaced. The only thing I still have is the Torah learning locked deep in my mind. It is something I will never relinquish as long as Hashem grants me time in this world."

# A Sojourn in the Night

THE COLLAPSE OF COMMUNISM was a highly significant event in contemporary history, and the *nissim* and *niflaos* that I saw in the Soviet Union can only be ascribed to the *ikvesa d'Mashicha*. It's not difficult to recall, however, a time when Jews in the Soviet Union were nothing less than hostages in body and soul, and the contrast between then and now is striking. What remains to be seen is the repercussions this political change will have on the fate of our brethren.

When I last visited Russia, there was overt oppression and persecution. Jews were kept under surveillance by the KGB, Torah study groups were held in small apartments with the shades drawn, and religious holy objects had to be concealed. There was a distinct air of menace everywhere. Even American Jews, carrying American passports with the proper visas and identification papers had to be cautious. At the behest of Agudas Yisrael of America, I traveled to the Soviet Union with my good friend and colleague, Rabbi Yoel Schonfeld, to bring *chizuk*, words of Torah, and the all-important *tefillin* and mezuzahs.

Arriving at customs in Moscow, we were asked to empty every one of our bags and spread everything out on a long table. Each article was examined meticulously by the customs officials. Even my tube of toothpaste was squeezed to make certain there were no secret messages inside. We were questioned closely: Why did we have two pairs of *tefillin*, what did we need so many mezuzahs for, what was the purpose of all the religious books, etc.? We managed, through some adroit answering, to deflect their suspicions, but there was one frightening moment when the official who was digging into my bags came across a *chalif* (a ritual slaughtering knife) I had wrapped in tissue to bring to a *shochet* in Leningrad. I knew the *chalif* would be the instrument for providing food to countless Jewish families for years to come. I watched anxiously as he felt it through the tissues, and then to my relief put it back.

When the nerve-racking search was finally completed, we were permitted to enter Moscow. There we found *Yidden* who were so gladdened by our presence that it was almost heartbreaking to witness their desperation for a *Yiddishe vort* or a friendly handshake. We distributed religious articles, conducted clandestine Torah study groups, and visited the different shuls. We also had the *zechus* to *daven* beside the Kopuster Rebbe's *kever*. But a slight tinge of danger colored everything we saw and did in the following stories.

Rav Yisrael Salanter once said that the mitzvos were so dear to him that even if the reward for doing *averos* were to go to *Gan Eden* and the punishment for doing mitzvos were to go to *Gehinnom*, he would still choose to do the mitzvos.

*Any mitzvah for which* klal Yisrael *was* moser nefesh *in times of danger will always survive.*

SHABBOS 130a

# Traveling Candlesticks

In addition to religious practice, Jewish culture was not permitted to exist under the Communists and the authorities clamped down hard on Jewish artists. They were forbidden to exhibit their works and they were denied the supplies they needed.

After staying in Kiev for a few days, one of the Jews we had befriended there informed us that a Jewish artist named Myla was being harrassed by the government and needed encouragement. He asked us to pay her a visit, and we arranged to go see her that very day.

Once we arrived at her building, we realized that we had not been given Myla's apartment number. We stood hesitantly outside for a moment until we saw a middle-aged woman about to enter. Approaching her, we asked for Mrs. Kurlansky.

The woman looked at us with a suspicious frown and asked brusquely, "Who wants her?"

Being cautious had become second nature to us in the USSR, and so we answered evasively, "Friends."

Back and forth it went until at last the woman, realizing

that we were not a threat, identified herself as Myla. She invited us to come up to her apartment, where she lived with her mother and husband. Once inside, Myla greeted her mother, whispered a few words to her, and then her mother went into the other room. We looked around; it was a very small and sparsely furnished flat, but clean and neat.

Myla invited us to have a seat then proceeded to pull out from every drawer, closet, shelf, and corner paintings, leatherwork, and artistic objects, while she explained, "This is something I completed a year ago. This is a work I made from clay..." She kept producing one after another.

We sat and admired everything. We realized how vital it was for her to have an audience, any audience, view and appreciate the fruits of her creativity. After the informal exhibition was over and we had finished enthusiastically praising her talent, she began telling us a little about what she was being forced to endure.

"I am not able to obtain art supplies — no paint, no canvas, no plaster. The worst part is that the works I have already created I must hide. They will not allow me to sell them or even to show them to anyone because I'm a Jew — for that reason alone. To be an artist is the only thing I know," she explained bitterly. "It's my life, my sustenance, the air I breathe. And they have taken it from me."

We sat in silence for a moment, not knowing what to say to give *chizuk* to this dispirited woman. I wanted very much to give her something — a tangible object perhaps that might lift her spirits and restore her zeal for life, something that might add meaning to her oppressed existence.

I took out of our bag two traveling candlestick holders and the last six remaining Shabbos candles. As I gave them to her, I said, "Myla, I know life is very hard for you. But I hope that lighting these candles will, from now on, bring joy and light into your life. May Hashem help you out of your difficulties very soon."

She appeared to be both moved and happy, as she held the candles in her hands. She smiled as she felt their smooth, glossy surface. It was as if she were expertly evaluating the perfection of their shape and form.

After a minute she said, "Rabbi, I would like to ask you something. I know one must light two candles every Friday night. This much I remember from my grandmother's house. But since I only have six candles, perhaps it would be permissible for me to light just one every Shabbos so that the candles will last six weeks instead of only three?"

I reflected for a while, and then thought back to a most interesting case noted among our *Acharonim*. A man in prison was told that he could select any day he wanted to be free to observe the mitzvos, but only for that day. His question was, which day should he choose — perhaps Yom Kippur or maybe the first day of Sukkos or Shavuos? The answer was that he should choose the very first day allowed, even an ordinary weekday. One reason is because when one has an opportunity to perform a mitzvah no time should be wasted in doing so. However, there is an even more profound reason for this. Each and every day we pray for the *geulah ha-sheleimah* — we hope the redemption will come each second, when no Jew will be a prisoner and every Jew will be allowed to perform the mitzvos freely. Therefore, we do not procrastinate. When the opportunity to fulfill a religious obligation presents itself, we must grab it. And so, I advised Myla to light the required two candles.

# The Last Page

The Archipova Street Shul in Moscow, where we went first, was a gray stone building with a short flight of stairs in front that led to a large, decorated sanctuary in the ornate Russian style. In its former glory, a few hundred congregants had *davened* there each Shabbos. Now there were less than a hundred men there.

We observed that, curiously enough, on Shabbos the congregation would break up into five or six separate *minyanim*. When we asked one old man the reason for this, he answered with a shrug, "What else can we do? Our lives are so uncertain. We never know where we'll be next Shabbos, so each one of us wants to make sure we get an *aliyah* on Shabbos."

When we *davened* in the Archipova Street Shul during the week, there were no more than twenty people there. They were mostly older men. Except for a growing group of young *ba'alei teshuvah*, most of the young people would not even come near the shul, lest they lose their jobs or student status.

That morning, as I sat *davening* on a hard wooden bench,
I noticed one wizened old man about eighty years old eyeing
me through his thick round glasses. Like many of the other
*Yidden* we had met, he looked poverty-stricken. I saw that he
held in his hand a piece of paper which he did not even glance
at, and his expression was soulful as he concentrated on each
word that he uttered. His eyes never left me throughout the
*davening*, however, and I could not fathom why he was so
mesmerized.

Afterwards, as I was putting away my *tallis* and *tefillin*, he
came over. Smiling nervously, he thrust out the single sheet
of paper I had noticed earlier and showed it to me. Then he
said, with heartbreaking sincerity, "*Zeh ha-siddur sheli* — This
is my *siddur.*"

The unspoken plea in his eyes was truly pitiful. I took the
piece of paper from his hand and looked at it. The only *tefillah*
printed on the slightly crumpled and worn page — obviously
the last remnant of some long-gone *siddur* — was the *Kaddish.*

We had only just arrived in Russia, and we had managed
to bring in with us only two *siddurim.* It was impossible to
predict when and under what circumstances there might arise
perhaps an even more imperative need for the *siddur.* Without
calculation, however, I put my *siddur* into his hands and said
to him, "*Zeh ha-siddur shelcha....*"

# *Threadbare*

In order to be permitted to remain in the Soviet Union and emerge unscathed at that time, it was absolutely essential to keep as low a profile as possible and not attract any undue attention. This was the course of action we followed throughout our stay in Russia, and it served us well. So it was to my consternation that while sitting in shul one morning, I heard my name being called repeatedly in a loud, booming voice. I turned around and saw a large, burly man, who bore an uncanny resemblance to Leonid Brezhnev, the premier of Russia at the time, walking down the aisle and announcing my name to the entire congregation.

He stopped at my seat and asked if I was the person he was seeking. Reluctantly I answered, "Yes, I am." He shook my hand vigorously, told me not to rush — that he would wait for me in back of the shul until I finished *daven*ing — and then he would escort me to see Reb Mottel, the *shochet*, about a serious matter.

I wondered who Reb Mottel the *shochet* was and what he could possibly want with me. I did not have long to speculate, however, for as soon as I finished, the man led me out a back door and into a narrow alley behind the shul. We walked through a twisting passageway for a short distance and came to a stop in front of a small house. There an old woman, wearing a *babushka*, sat on a stool plucking the feathers off a chicken. My companion knocked loudly on the door and it was quickly opened, as if the occupant had been standing right behind it, waiting for our signal.

Reb Mottel practically pulled me inside the house, which I saw was a type of office. In his mid-sixties, he was small and slight, but spry. His greeting was friendly, but I was admonished in a whisper, as he held his finger to his lips, to stay very quiet. He bolted the door securely behind me and then, without saying anything and in a furtive manner, climbed on a chair and took something down from the top shelf of a large closet standing in the corner. I saw it was a large box, and out of it he took a brand-new *kapote*.

He explained that he had heard through the underground Jewish network that I knew how to check a garment for *shatnez*. "Would you be so kind as to check this for me?" he asked hopefully, as he proffered the long, black coat.

I answered, "It would be my privilege," and sat down with the coat. As I began to check it, Reb Mottel hovered nearby, looking anxiously over my shoulder. The moment I finished checking one area, he asked eagerly, "Is it good?"

I answered affirmatively and Reb Mottel broke into a joyous little dance. Each area of the coat that I checked and found without *shatnez* elicited the same intensely happy reaction from Reb Mottel, and I wondered about it. Why was this making him so inordinately ecstatic? Finally I finished, handed him his *kapote*, and told him that there was no problem in wearing the garment.

When he heard this, Reb Mottel leapt with joy into the air. He literally lifted me to my feet, gave me a hug and kiss, and amidst a profusion of thanks and blessings I took my leave.

On the way back to the shul, his friend told me that Reb Mottel had been wearing a tattered and threadbare *kapote* for as long as he could remember. The new one had lain unworn in his closet for seven years — he had refused to wear it until it had been checked for *shatnez*.

Reb Mottel in his home.

# *Hunger Strike*

W̲e were told by one of the *Yidden* in shul to look up Reb Feivel in particular, and try to help him in whatever way we could, as it was a well-known fact that he was on the verge of starvation. At *daven*ing the next day, we asked someone to point him out. He showed us a little old man with a full white beard, wearing a long frock coat and sitting by himself in a corner looking into a *Chumash*. He was painfully thin and his appearance was like that of a holy relic from some long vanished time — a time when a vibrant Jewish life still existed in Russia, a time that had passed Reb Feivel by and left him for all intents alone.

We went over and told him who we were. He gave us a courteous nod and solemnly shook our hands. Then I took out the vacuum-packed cans of food we had brought along with us from America and handed them to him.

"Reb Feivel," I said in Yiddish, "this is for you." He

looked at the cans with surprise and pushed them gently back into my hands, trying to be polite.

"*Nein, nein. Ich darf es nisht* — No, no. I don't need it."

Again I tried to give him the food, entreating him to take it, explaining that we had brought it especially for him.

Again he pushed it back into my hands and said no, he didn't want it.

We could not understand why Reb Feivel was refusing the food so adamantly. Perhaps he thought we would not have any food to eat if we gave him ours, or perhaps...

Suddenly it occurred to me why Reb Feivel was turning down our food. "Reb Feivel," I exclaimed, "*es iz* glatt kosher!"

He thought for a moment about what I had just told him and then his face became wreathed in a broad smile. "Glatt kosher?" he said. "Then I will take it for Shabbos."

Reb Feivel in shul.

After Yaakov dreamed about the angels climbing and descending the ladder to Heaven, the Torah states that Yaakov awoke and began to *daven*.

On the other hand, when Paroh awoke from his dream about the seven fat and skinny cows, what did he do? He rolled over on his other side and went back to sleep.

From this, Reb Aharon M'Karlin pointed out the difference between Yaakov and Paroh.

When Yaakov awoke from sleep, his immediate waking moments were spent doing the *avodah* of Hashem: *Modeh Ani, negel vasser, Birchos Ha-shachar.* Conversely, upon awakening, Paroh's immediate reaction was to go back to sleep. Thus, it is no wonder that when a Jew emerges from spiritual slumber, he immediately tries to serve Hashem.

# Ex Nihilo

eter Mann caught my attention the moment he entered the Archipova Street Shul. For one thing, he was not dressed in typical Muscovite attire, so I assumed he was probably a visitor. For another, he was half the age of anyone else there. He had brought along his wife and seven-year-old son, and that was also very unusual. His wife went into the ladies' section, and he went to the back of the shul to request a pair of *tefillin*. I watched as he very carefully donned the *tefillin* and sat down to *daven*. After shul, I struck up a conversation with him.

We introduced ourselves and Peter explained that he was a mathematician living in East Berlin. He had been asked to come as a consultant to a large concern based in Russia. I was a little surprised. What a unique individual this must be! To be a Jew living in Germany, which was practically devoid of Jews, must be hard. To live in a Communist Germany must be even more difficult. But to live as a religious Jew in such an atheistic and spiritual wasteland was really extraordinary. I was eager to know more about Peter Mann and his family, and we arranged to meet in the park later to talk further.

It was a brisk and windy day, as Peter, his wife Babbo, and his son Johannes and I sat on a bench in the park. I asked Peter how he came to be living in East Berlin. He answered almost as if he were apologizing, "My family has lived in Germany for generations. My great-grandfather was one of the founders of the Reform Movement. During the war, my parents were fortunate. They got out in time. But when the war ended, they came back to live. Berlin had been their home for generations. Then, of course, the Wall went up and they were trapped there. Even if they had wanted to leave, they no longer could."

Listening to Peter's story, I could not imagine how he had discovered his religious roots. From whom had he learned to *daven* and put on *tefillin?* From what deep recesses in his soul had he felt the desire to do so? The members of his family had most likely not practiced Judaism for generations, and any remnant of Jewry left in Germany could hardly have ignited his religiosity. I encouraged him to continue.

"About five years ago I simply began feeling that something important was missing in my life. I knew I was a Jew, but I didn't know exactly what that meant. I knew there was some type of heritage, but I could not imagine what it was. I began to read the New Testament; it was the only Bible I could find in German. But after going through it, I felt dissatisfied, incomplete. I knew if there was a New Testament, there had to be an Old one. But how could I read it? I did not know any Hebrew. I found a professor who taught Semitic languages in the university I had attended. I asked him to teach me Hebrew, and he agreed, but only on one condition: that I sign a document agreeing not to use my knowledge for religious purposes.

"The unvarnished and pure truth of what I was learning became more and more evident to me as I continued my studies. Eventually I began to *daven* every day. Now my wife and I are trying to ensure that our son will learn about his birthright.''

Peter's account touched me profoundly. How indomitable was the Jewish spirit. How awesome that years and generations of ignorance and neglect were unable to vanquish it. With no assistance, with no encouragement, and, in fact, against all odds, Peter and his family had become true *chozrim b'teshuvah.*

I asked Peter if there was anything I could do to help him. ''Yes, Rabbi. If nothing else, we desperately need religious books in Germany. The books are the keys to our survival.''

I assured him that I would try my best to see to it that this need was filled. We exchanged addresses and made plans to keep in touch.

*Epilogue:*

When I returned to the United States, I immediately sent a package to Peter and his family containing books and children's tapes for little Johannes. Then I didn't hear from Peter for a while. Before Rosh Hashanah, however, I received a special delivery letter from East Berlin. It was Peter asking that I call him immediately about an urgent matter. When he came to the phone, he sounded frustrated and got right to the point.

''There is no one here, Rabbi, who is able to conduct the services for the High Holy Days,'' he said. ''I was asked to do it, but truthfully I'm not sure that I am capable enough yet. There is so much I don't know.''

I understood and appreciated his dilemma and told him not to despair. I would send him *machzorim* and detailed instructions on what to do. Through a publisher friend, *machzorim* with German translation were sent, and Peter wrote a while later that everything had gone well.

When Agudas Yisrael was made aware of the need for Jewish outreach in Germany, emmissaries were sent to East Berlin and Peter Mann became the official conduit to the small vestige of Jews living there. Eventually Peter and his family received a visa and left East Berlin for Strassburg, where he joined a *kollel.*

**Peter, Babbo, and Johannes Mann.**

*Baruch...ha-gomel chasadim tovim l'amo Yisrael....*

Rav Avigdor Miller *shlita* points out that it sounds redundant to call a *chesed* good. Aren't all *chasadim* good? By its very definition, a chesed means a favor, a kindness. Nevertheless, the *pasuk* praises Hashem for granting us favors that are good.

We realize, therefore, that not only does Hashem do that which is good for each individual, but He customizes it to suit the needs and wants of the person. For instance, fruits come in different colors and have various textures and flavors. In other words, they are designed to appeal to each person's own taste and appetite. Likewise, the favors Hashem bestows upons us have been tailor-made to whatever is needed or wanted by the human being. Thus, we thank and praise Him for showing us *chesed* that is good, i.e., exactly suited to us.

# It Happened in Heaven

In Leningrad we stayed at the Nationale Hotel. It was governmentally approved, highly recommended by Intourist,* and, "by coincidence," the only one in which we were permitted to stay. The place was spartan, dreary, and functional at best, but as soon as we checked in we realized why we had been instructed to go there. The reservation clerk at the front desk immediately took away our passports and glared at us while we signed our names in the registration book. She asked some very pointed questions about our itinerary: Where would we be spending our day? When would we be returning? Whom would we be meeting? The persistent and sustained questioning unnerved us with its implicit warning: Go only where you're supposed to go; be only where you say you'll be. She perused our bogus schedule of visits to cultural attractions and then looked suspiciously back to us. Finally, with a curt nod, she told us to go upstairs to our room and unpack. As soon as we arrived on our floor, we were startled to see another

---

* the official government tourist agency

woman standing in the hall, watching us unlock the door of our room and carry in our bags Then we knew beyond a shadow of a doubt that we would be kept under strict and constant surveillance. We also knew that the need for extreme caution that we had been warned about in the States had not been exaggerated.

Our contact in Leningrad was Yitzchak Cohen, and he had arranged a meeting for us that evening with some young professionals. The gathering was to take place in a high-rise apartment building in the center of the city, where we were to teach a *Chumash* class. Leaving the hotel under the watchful eyes of the desk clerk and floor matron, we concealed our *Chumashim* under our jackets and walked out as unobtrusively as possible.

Arriving at the pre-arranged apartment building, we knocked on the door very softly and only once, so as not to attract the neighbors' attention. It was quickly opened, and we were hastily ushered inside. To our delight, almost thirty people had gathered for the meeting, where only five or six had been expected. A few friendly words of greeting were then exchanged. They appeared to be a highly intelligent group and seemed eager for us to begin the class.

One young man, in particular, seemed to stand out from the rest. He was frail looking with a trimmed beard, and his eyes, behind wire-rimmed glasses, regarded us with a great deal of appreciative warmth. The young man introduced himself. His name was Sasha, he was a doctor, and he lived nearby. As we conversed, Sasha's sensitive countenance and soft-spoken manner signified to me a highly refined inner being.

After all the introductions had been made, the learning session began. True, there were only two *Chumashim* for thirty students, but there was such electrified enthusiasm and zealousness in the learning that it seemed to link every mind and

100

soul into one body. We began to expound on the *pasukim* in *Parashas Ekev*, and even those who could not follow the actual text avidly participated in the intensive discussion. The back-and-forth, questions and answers, comments and remarks flew. Unfortunately, so did the time.

I looked at my watch and saw it was 10:30. I nudged Reb Yoel, and although our students were completely engrossed in an excited give-and-take on a Rashi, I pointed out the time. Yoel nodded as if to say, "Let's go." We both knew that to be caught in the street or coming into the hotel after 11:00 would put us into a very awkward, if not outright dangerous, position. So we stopped the discussion reluctantly, said good-night to everyone, and got up to go. But as I stood with my hand on the doorknob, Sasha came rushing over to me. He put his hand on my arm and, with urgency in his voice, pleaded: "*Od chamesh dakos* — five more minutes."

I felt myself in a quandary. What was to be done? It was getting late. The sensible course of action would be to leave now. On the other hand, the complete sincerity and profound longing in his request were preventing us from doing the sensible thing.

We sat down once again and began learning, this time with an even greater measure of fervor. It was truly a *zechus* to be teaching them. Their rapt attention to every syllable we uttered and their resoluteness to comprehend every nuance of every letter was inspiring. I was not sure at that point who was gleaning more from our lesson — the students or the teachers.

Time passed quickly, and I realized that it was now almost 11:30. Once again we got up to leave and said our goodbyes. No sooner did we walk to the door, however, then Sasha was there barring our way. This time he grabbed my arm and looked imploringly into my eyes. He said once more, "*Od chamesh dakos* — five more minutes."

I didn't know how to respond. I knew good judgment dictated that we leave immediately. But I felt torn. How could we leave when we were being entreated so? On the other hand, how could we not when we knew that our safe return depended on it? Who knew when we would ever have another opportunity to fortify the *Yiddishe neshamos* in this group? On the other hand, who knew what would happen to us when we returned to our hotel so many hours past curfew? My rational thinking told me to refuse; my heart told me I could not.

We sat down once again and continued learning. When we finished, one of the participants, a doctor from Vilna, went over to the piano that was standing in a corner of the living room and begged us to teach him a few *niggunim*. We sang a few notes and in a minute everyone in the room was on their feet, singing and dancing to the music. The merit of the holy words of Torah learned that night and that of the holy *niggunim* being sung must surely have acted as a safeguard. For, amazingly, none of the neighbors banged on the door, complained about the noise, nor summoned the secret police. After a while, we insisted that we truly had to leave.

As my companion and I stood up, Sasha stood also and said, "Before you go, Rabbis, I would like to say that I cannot thank you enough for what you have given us tonight. Allow me to express a small measure of our gratitude by inviting you to a farewell *seudah* at my home tomorrow at noon." We were touched by his gesture and accepted Sasha's invitation gladly.

"It would be an honor for us to attend," we replied. Then, after bidding everyone good night, we left without further delay and walked out into one of the famed white nights of Leningrad.

Although it was well after midnight, the streets were as bright as day. We felt vulnerable and more than a little frightened, not knowing what lay in store for us at our hotel or even around the next street corner, for that matter. Nevertheless, the spiritual uplifting we received this evening made the trepidations we felt insignificant and of minor consequence.

Back at our hotel, we found the desk clerk with her head down on the desk, fast asleep, and the floor matron likewise asleep at her post. We tiptoed past, and with heartfelt thanks to Hashem for His protection, slipped quietly into our room.

The next day was damp and gray, but suffused with a surprisingly gentle warmth. We *davened* and learned for a while in the Leningrad Shul and then returned to our hotel to prepare for our visit to Sasha's apartment.

I had decided to bring along a gift as a token of our appreciation for the farewell meal and as an acknowledgment of our respect and affection. The flight bag that had served as a hiding place for the religious articles we had smuggled in was almost empty, but as I dug my hand into the bag, I pulled out a *tallis*. This might be a good gift, I thought. Sasha is a young man; he'll be a *chasan* soon and will need a *tallis*.

For some reason, though, I didn't think it was the right thing to give him and put it back. I felt in the bag again and this time came up with a *Kiddush* cup. Again, inexplicably, I felt it was not appropriate and put it back.

Once more, I stuck my hand into the bag and this time I pulled out a challah cover. It was made of white terylene, had a light blue *Magen David* embroidered on it, and across the front in blue were the Hebrew words *Shabbat Shalom*. For some reason I thought, This one or the other is it — the perfect gift for Sasha. I put the challah cover in a brown paper bag and hid it under my jacket as we left the hotel.

Arriving at Sasha's apartment at exactly 12:00, we were astounded to see that not only were most of the participants of the previous night's lecture present, but so too were at least a dozen new people. Everyone seemed happy to see us and greeted us warmly. A large sign hanging on the wall was hand-lettered with the words *mazel tov*. The table bore a large array of delicacies which had been arranged with obvious care. In the center, in a place of prominence, was one single *shemurah matzah*, which had probably been carefully preserved for a special occasion since the last Pesach. A crystal wine bottle, with about two inches of wine in it, had a sticker pasted on that read *"yayin mi-Yerushalayim."* There were some vegetables, a few cut-up fruits, and little squares of cake. Very hospitably, everyone urged us, "Please sit, have something..."

We hesitated. We were reluctant to partake of the meal, for it was obvious that much of this generous spread had been hoarded and sparingly doled out over the past year. When or how would these people ever again have the opportunity to replenish their meager stock? We realized, however, how offended our host would have been had we refused to eat anything, so we sat down and joined everyone at the table. The meal progressed splendidly, with animated conversation and congenial banter. We were aware — even then — that the camaraderie and warmth we felt on that special Leningrad afternoon in that small, spare Leningrad apartment was of the sort we would savor for the rest of our lives.

When Sasha got up to serve the next course, I followed him into the kitchen. I wanted to present his gift to him in private, since I had not brought a gift for everyone, though they certainly deserved it. As Sasha busied himself at the stove, I walked over and, handing him the present, said, "Sasha, this is for you."

He seemed taken aback, and in almost a disapproving manner thrust the paper bag back into my hands. I handed it to him again and said, "Sasha, *zeh matanah* for you." He looked very surprised and flustered, but this time he took the bag.

I watched as he opened it, took out the challah cover and unfolded it slowly. Then, after taking one look at it, Sasha burst into tears. I felt bewildered and just stood there for a moment, not knowing what to say or how to react. After a few seconds, Sasha composed himself and wordlessly led me out of the kitchen and down the hall into a small vestibule, where there stood a tall bookcase with some old crumbling *sefarim* on the top shelf. Sasha climbed up on a stepladder and took out something very carefully from between two tall volumes.

"You don't know how long I've hoped for this," he said to me. Then he bent over and handed me what he had just taken out.

It was a thin, white folded paper napkin. I slowly opened it up and looked at it. There on the front was drawn in blue marker a *Magen David*, and across the top in the same blue ink was written in Hebrew *Shabbat Shalom*.

Sasha took the challah cover I had given him, folded it up, and placed it between the two *sefarim*. He climbed down the stepladder, and pointing to the napkin I was holding in my hand, said softly to me, "This one is for you."

The *Ribbono shel Olam* had not only chosen the exact *matanah* Sasha was to receive, but even its color and design. This paper napkin is among my most precious possessions.

*R' Nachman bar Yitzchak says: Whoever causes a chasan to rejoice it is as if he has rebuilt one of the ruins of Yerushalayim.*

BERACHOS 6a

Why does it not simply say "he has rebuilt Yerushalayim" instead of "the ruins of Yerushalayim"?

The answer is that in order for the *Beis Ha-mikdash* to be rebuilt, first the old foundations must be relaid. Thus, we can see that the old influences add on to the new. The fresh foundation laid when a marriage takes place reconstructs the ancient groundwork necessary for the rebuilding of the *Beis Ha-mikdash* itself. Is it any wonder that a Jew cherishes the past?

# Heart of Stone

The final leg of our journey through Russia was Kiev. Here the feeling of melancholy and uneasiness that had been everywhere was even more pronounced. Even the Jews we met seemed to regard us with suspicion at first. The weather was always dismal, drizzly and gray, and a fine mist hung in the air almost constantly. The morning of our arrival we *davened* in the Kiev Shul. It was large — almost cavernous — but practically empty, for there were only thirteen or fourteen *mispallelim* there.

After *davening*, we went out into the street to call our contact in Kiev, Eliyahu Landinsky, whose name and number we had been given in the States. The phone in our hotel room was most surely bugged — at least in the street at a random phone booth there was a chance that our conversation would be private.

After identifying ourselves to Reb Eliyahu, he told us to meet him in one half hour at a park in the center of the city.

He said we would find him sitting on a bench to the right of the entrance.

Following Reb Eliyahu's directions, we arrived at our rendezvous at the prearranged time. There on the bench we saw a thin, distinguished-looking man, about seventy-five years old, with fine-boned features and snow white hair. He held himself rigid, as though in a state of tense expectation, and kept looking in every direction. As we approached, the expression on Reb Eliyahu's face became more relaxed, and his eyes looked welcoming. He seemed pleased to see us. We sat down on the bench next to him, and after an exchange of greetings, Reb Eliyahu began telling us in Yiddish how difficult life was in Russia for the Jews. He described the desperate straits in which most Jews existed, and it was evident from the slight quavering in his voice as he spoke that the situation pained him greatly. His attitude toward his own circumstances was concerned, but accepting.

Reb Eliyahu explained that for the past twenty years he had been traveling around the Soviet Union collecting money for the restoration and maintenance of the *mekomos ha-kedoshim* there. In addition, he had personally assumed the task of *shomer* and caretaker of the *kevarim*, and with his own hands tended the graves. Without a doubt, he told us, the Secret Police took an avid interest in his activities. Listening to R' Eliyahu speak of his life, we knew he possessed steel-like determination and unflinching courage, for without these traits his life would surely have been intolerable.

After we spoke for a short while, Reb Eliyahu got up and told us to meet him in the same spot the next morning. He said he had something to give us. We parted with expressions of mutual pleasure at our having met and separately made our way out of the park and back to our hotel. We were intrigued by Reb Eliyahu's last remark that he would be giving us something, but could not imagine what it would be, and so we anxiously awaited our next appointment.

The following day dawned a bit more brightly, but was bitingly cold. We *davened* early in the Kiev Shul, ate breakfast, and hurried off to our meeting. Although we arrived a couple of minutes ahead of schedule, Reb Eliyahu was already waiting for us on the bench. We sat down next to him and, without preamble, he turned to us and said in Yiddish, "What I give you now is something very very special. They will try to take it from you. Hide it; make sure that you hide it well. Perhaps they will not find it, and you will be able to bring it home with you." He reached into his pocket and brought out a smooth stone, light tan in color and about the size of a small egg. He placed it in my hand carefully, with reverence. My fingers closed tightly around it. I did not know what the significance of the stone was, but I was sure it was no ordinary rock. I waited expectantly for Reb Eliyahu's explanation.

His face was grave, and there was a note of pride in his voice as he said: "This stone is from the *kever* of the *heilige* Baal Shem Tov." He paused a moment as his eyes searched mine to see if I fully appreciated the import of what he had told me about the stone's origin. My face must have revealed the awe I felt, for Reb Eliyahu looked pleased. Then again he warned, "Remember to hide it; hide it well. If they find it, they will take it from you."

I took the precious stone that had lain for hundreds of years at the final resting place of one of the greatest *tzaddikim* that had ever lived and inserted it deep inside my pocket. I felt overwhelmed by the privilege of having it in my possession. I thought about the strong *kesher* between a Jew and his past. I thought about how inextricably each generation is linked and bound to the one before, and how powerful is their yearning to feel and see something tangible that will reconnect them in some way to their never-to-be-forgotten or relinquished ancestry. I had already started wondering where to place this stone when I returned home, how to appropriately display it, and how uplifting an influence it would exert on those who saw and touched it.

I was jarred from my reverie when Reb Eliyahu cautioned me almost sternly once again before leaving, "Remember, hide the stone well. If they find it they will take it..."

While packing to leave, I made certain to hide the stone Reb Eliyahu had given me in the bottom of a separate zippered bag, which I concealed under a pile of clothes in a corner of my suitcase. At the airport, the customs official was grim and very tough. She went through all my possessions with such thoroughness, it was as if she were determined to find something incriminating. She peered into every bag and case, and took out every personal item. It was disconcerting, to say the least, to have one's things pulled apart in so rough and peremptory a manner. But I remained silent, hoping she would not detain me for any trumped-up reason and praying she would not discover the stone.

Just as I thought she was finally finished ransacking my things and that I would be permitted to repack and board my plane, she grabbed the travel kit in which the stone was hidden, unzipped it and rifled through the few personal items inside. After a minute, she began to scream, "The stone, the stone." My heart stopped. I saw she was holding the stone in her hand.

I heard Reb Eliyahu's voice in my head warning me again and again. "Hide it well; if they find it they will take it," and I knew then with awful certainty that they would take the stone. The customs official called out loudly and abrasively in Russian, her tone of voice urgent. No less than three officers in green uniforms came rushing over. They took one look at the stone in the official's hand, and then all four stalked off to a private room nearby. After a couple of minutes they emerged and, while the other officers hovered in the background, my customs official came over and said harshly, "You know, you're not permitted to take stones from a cemetery in Russia." There was a silent pause. They were all staring icily at me, scanning my expression. "Of course, you understand you will *not* be taking this stone," she said with grim satisfaction.

The enormity of my disappointment was suffocating, but I tried to appear casual and said, in what I felt was a matter-of-fact tone, "It's a stone."

Again she repeated more strongly, "You understand you will *not* be taking this stone with you."

Again I could only answer, "It's a stone." But even as I said it, I knew it would no longer be mine.

The customs official, with the stone still clutched tightly in her hand, walked away. I have no idea what she did with that precious and palpable momento of our people's holy past, but this heartrending loss pains me to this very day.

# In the Land of the Living

On another occasion, Eliyahu Landinsky promised to take us to some famous *kevarim*, and we arranged to meet at the Kiev Shul in the morning. Reb Eliyahu was not there when we arrived, but a few minutes later we noticed him come in. He towered over everyone — he was over six feet tall — and we rushed over to greet him. To our surprise, he turned away and acted as if he didn't know us. When *davening* was over, however, he whispered that he would speak to us outside.

Away from all the prying eyes and ears, a bit of his former warmth returned and we arranged to meet at 5:00 A.M. the following day in the shul. From there, Reb Eliyahu said, he would take us to the cemetery.

The next day, at the appointed time and in the appointed place, we sat and waited for Reb Eliyahu, but he did not come. We waited and waited, but still he did not come. We didn't want to think about what could have detained him, so we decided to try again the following day, unfortunately with the same results. For the next two days, we rushed eagerly over to the *shul* in the pre-dawn darkness, only to be disappointed. By this time we were becoming concerned for his safety; we were losing hope of ever again seeing Eliyahu Landinsky or the holy sites. Since we had to catch a plane back to the States right after Shabbos, we resolved to give it one more try. We trudged through the dark once more that early Friday morning, along the damp streets and into the deserted shul, waiting silently there for what seemed like a long time.

Suddenly we heard the sound of a car engine and then footsteps quickly approaching. The door was flung open, and there stood Reb Eliyahu. His expression was worried, but all he said in explanation was, "*Ich hub tzorres tzruros* — I have terrible troubles." He did not elaborate.

Leading us outside, where two cars were waiting, he motioned for us to quickly get into one of the cars, which was driven by a young man in a sweatsuit, while he got into the other car with another driver. Our car followed Reb Eliyahu's, and as we sped along the Russian highway, dawn was just beginning to break.

My thoughts were a jumble. Where had Reb Eliyahu been all this time? Why did he seem so worried? Why were we in two separate cars? We didn't know what to make of the situation, but we did know one thing. Eliyahu Landinsky had been *moser nefesh* to bring us here today.

The car pulled up to the cemetery gates. We jumped out, and as Reb Eliyahu got out of his car, he indicated that we were to follow him. We walked behind him while he showed us tombstone after tombstone of well-known *Yidden* who had long since passed away, but on whose merits we still relied to help us through this world. We stopped to say *Tehillim* at the *kevarim* of the Skverer Rebbes and felt that every word we recited there was imbued with a special intensity and dimension of meaning.

Eliyahu Landinsky showing us some famous *kevarim.*

Finally Reb Eliyahu turned to us and said, "*Ir darft gein yetzt* — you must go now." We started to leave, but then I noticed that Reb Eliyahu was not following.

"Aren't you coming?" I asked.

"Not right now," he answered, and I could see his face looked drawn, weary, and resigned. "Go without me," he said. "Go now."

I ran back and kissed him. I thanked him for bringing us and I thanked him on behalf of all *klal Yisrael* for being such a staunch guardian of our people's ancestry. I felt reluctant to leave this old man all by himself here in this loneliest of places. But again he urged me, "*Gei. Gei.*"

I started to leave again. Then I ran back to hug him once more. I wanted Reb Eliyahu to fully realize how much I — we all — appreciated what he was doing and had done. He smiled

114

at me and as I turned to leave — as if *he* were consoling *me* — he said, "I will be *mispallel* and you be *mispallel,* and maybe somewhere in the middle our *tefillos* will meet...and so will we."

In Russia, any Jew's tenacious and unyielding adherence to the mitzvos and *minhagim* of their ancestors could only be the result of *ma'aseh avos siman l'banim.* Which of us does not take for granted our ability to eat kosher, to put on *tefillin,* or to *daven* with a *minyan?* The *Yidden* we met in Russia were willing to put aside their own safety, comfort and convenience in order to perform even one mitzvah. The self-sacrifice and untainted purity of their *neshamos* was of such a high level that it has remained an enduring inspiration.

*Etz chaim hi la'machazikim bah....*

MISHLEI 3:18

Be scrupulous about at least one mitzvah in your lifetime.

A person hurtling down the rapids is about to go over the edge of a huge waterfall, when he grabs onto a branch of a tree. That branch helps him pull himself away from the brink. So, too, a person should always be attached to at least one mitzvah in particular throughout his lifetime and punctilious in its observance, for that is his branch of salvation.

# Sold!

eb Chaim was a beloved fixture in our shul. Wrinkled and bent with age though he was, the rapport he enjoyed with the members who were far removed from him by time and life experience was astonishing. It was touching to see that when Reb Chaim shuffled slowly into shul on Shabbos, one young man would invariably accompany him to his seat, hovering over him until he was settled in his chair. The young men eagerly and attentively listened to his stories about the boyhood pranks he pulled off while growing up in the tiny *shtetl* of Troki in Lithuania. Moreover, the genuine affection everyone felt for him was heartily reciprocated by Reb Chaim and contributed to the warmth and *achdus* of our congregation.

Although Reb Chaim was a modest and unassuming man, there was one *kibbud* he enjoyed and eagerly looked forward to receiving — being called to the Torah for *Maftir*. Every *Yid* appreciates receiving an *aliyah* to the Torah and considers it an honor. But for some reason, Reb Chaim felt a

117

particularly strong attachment to the *Haftarah*. As soon as his name was called, his face would become wreathed in smiles and he would walk as quickly as he could to the *bimah* to take his place. As he pronounced the *berachos* in a loud, clear voice, the expression on his face was beatific. His whole being emanated with joy when he finished reading the *Haftarah* and was told *yashar koach* by all those who stood nearby. "It's one of the greatest pleasures in my life," he often replied.

One morning in late May, Reb Chaim arrived at shul a little earlier than usual. In one hand he carried a large square package which he handed to the *gabbai*, explaining, "This is a present for the shul." The *gabbai* tore open the brown paper and inside was a beautifully bound *sefer*. The *sefer* was a collection of all the *Haftaros* that are read throughout the year. Reb Chaim beamed with pride as everyone in the shul admired it.

We expressed our pleasure at receiving such a special volume. We all knew that Reb Chaim subsisted on a meager pension and realized that the *sefer* had cost what was for him a great deal of money. Obviously his love for the *Haftarah* had impelled him to make this sacrifice.

That year, Reb Chaim called the president of the shul before Rosh Hashanah and asked to buy a seat for the upcoming *Yamim Noraim*. This would be the first year Reb Chaim would be *daven*ing with us for the High Holy Days. For the past fifty years, he had been *daven*ing in a shul that had closed recently.

On Yom Kippur, towards *Minchah* time, the *gabbai* was auctioning the *aliyos*. One by one, they were sold to the highest bidder, as is the custom in every *shul*, until finally the most important *aliyah* of the year was about to be auctioned: *Maftir Yonah*. Reb Chaim was practically on the edge of his seat, as he called out the first bid in a voice tremulous with excitement. Perhaps until now, the *aliyah* had been sold to the wealthiest member where he used to *daven*, and perhaps now

Reb Chaim thought he might have a chance to buy this special *aliyah*. That is, if his bid were successful, for as the bidding continued, to Reb Chaim's dismay, one or two members of the shul began bidding against him. The amounts being called out rose higher and higher, until Reb Chaim, with a deep sigh of disappointment, was forced to concede. He could not bid any higher, and he sat back in his seat, defeated. Immediately, one of the young men who had been bidding against him and had bought the *aliyah* came running over to Reb Chaim from across the shul.

"Reb Chaim," he called smilingly, "don't look so disappointed. We only bid for the *aliyah* to buy it for you. It's our privilege to give you *Maftir Yonah* as a token of our deep respect and appreciation."

Reb Chaim's eyes lit up and then brimmed with tears. I will admit mine did too. Their thoughtfulness was deeply touching. He looked around the shul. Everyone was smiling at him.

An awed hush filled the shul as Reb Chaim slowly made his way to the *bimah*, almost as if he were reluctant to get there too quickly lest this triumphal moment would pass too soon. The *sefer* he had given the shul lay open on the table, and he began reading from it in a clear and feeling voice, word by loving word. Never had I heard the cherished story of *Yonah* read with such expression and emotion. Everyone was riveted.

When he finished, Reb Chaim walked back to his seat, receiving gratefully the handshakes and blessings offered. I will never forget the complete contentment on his face, almost as though he had just experienced the culmination of his life's dreams.

Two days later, right before Sukkos, the family in whose basement Reb Chaim lived, informed us that he had returned his pure and precious *neshamah* to *Ha-kadosh Baruch Hu.*

Rabbi Samson Raphael Hirsch points out that the Hebrew root *nun-ches-mem* has a dual meaning: "to comfort" and "to alter one's thinking." We see the latter connotation in the *pasuk* concerning Hashem's anger with Noach's generation: "*Nichamti*," He declares. "I regret having made man" (*Bereshis* 6:7), meaning that Hashem changed His mind, as it were.

The act of *nichum aveilim* is, therefore, a way of changing the mourner's emotional state from depression to renewed hope.

# *One Good Turn*

Ann had been born and raised in Pennsylvania. When she married, she moved to San Francisco, and had not returned to the East for more than two decades. So her visit to New York City was exciting.

Her sister and brother-in-law, with whom she was staying, were anxious to show her around town and she enjoyed doing the conventional tourist-type things that most visitors to the city do. On her last Sunday in New York, she ventured alone to the Lower East Side to do some shopping. It seemed to Ann as if nothing had changed on Delancey Street. The tenements were still the same run-down, seedy buildings they were twenty years ago. The sidewalk vendors still hawked their wares loudly and abrasively. The shopowners still expected a good haggle over the price, and the crowds of shoppers, eager for a bargain, were thick as ever.

Ann turned down a small side street to get some relief from being jostled by the throng and as she walked along, she glanced idly into the store windows. She had almost passed a small Judaica shop when something in the window caught her eye. She came to an abrupt halt, then went closer to take a better look. There on display was a beautiful Torah mantle. It was made of maroon velvet and had a silver menorah embroidered on the front. There were also some Hebrew words embroidered in thin silver threads under the menorah, which because of Ann's lack of Hebrew education, she was unable to read.

She rushed into the shop and began questioning the clerk. "Did the Torah mantle in the window once belong to someone?" Where did it come from? How old was it? Was it for sale?

The clerk reacted defensively to Ann's questions. What concern was it of hers where the mantle had come from? No, it was definitely not for sale. Was she interested in buying something else? If not, then would she please leave. The salesclerk practically pushed Ann out of the store.

That evening, Ann, who was a close friend of my mother, telephoned and related the whole bizarre incident. I listened, but could not understand why the Torah mantle was so important to her until I heard her story.

"It was almost at the end of World War II. My brother Nochum had just turned eighteen, and my parents lived in dread that he would be called up. There was the draft then, you know. They took any and every able-bodied man. My brother was a very gentle and sensitive boy. He didn't even know how to raise his voice. He was the apple of my father's eye and my parents' only son. I remember how my mother checked the mail every day, terrified that there would be a draft notice. Finally one day it came. After that, it wasn't long before we were all standing — my parents, my sister, and I — on the pier in New York harbor, watching his ship sail for Europe. We cried as we waved goodbye, and I'll never forget how small he looked, standing at the railing, smiling bravely as he waved back with one hand, while his other hand clutched his *tefillin* bag.

"After that we woke up every morning anxiously wondering how he was. One Thursday, only a few months after he had left, we stopped wondering. The telegram came in the afternoon: 'The United States government regrets to inform you that your son, Nathan...' It was a big blow to my parents. They never really got over it. His loss was bad enough, but what made it almost impossible for them was the fact that they had nothing left to remember him by. All his things, including his *tefillin*, had been destroyed by the bomb that took his life. My parents were devastated.

"A few months after he died, they ordered a Torah mantle made for our community shul and had it inscribed with my brother's name. At least then they would have something that was Nochum's — something they could touch which belonged to him and would be a tangible reminder that once there was a boy — Nochum Jacobs. My parents have long since passed away, but I remember how much that Torah mantle meant to them. I remember how my father cried each time he kissed it.

"My sister and I married and moved away and I haven't seen the mantle in twenty-five years. I don't know how it came to be in that shop window, Rabbi. I could not read the Hebrew lettering, so I'm not even sure it *was* our mantle. But please, go down there and see if it's the one that belonged to our family. No matter what the price, we'll pay it. If it's ours, please get it back for us."

I agreed to investigate the origin of the mantle, took down her brother's and father's full Hebrew names, and then reassured Ann that if it would be within my power to do so, I would retrieve her family's cherished heirloom.

A heavy snow fell the next morning, and it was very cold

as I made my way down that evening to the Lower East Side. I found the Judaica store very easily with Ann's directions, but when I looked in the window, my expectation of quickly resolving the matter was diminished. In the window there was a display of a few popular children's books, some cassette tapes, and an array of lucite and enamel mezuzah cases, but no Torah mantle.

I went into the store, and the saleswoman came over to ask if she could be of any help. I explained that I had come to inquire about the Torah mantle that had been in the window the day before. The woman began to fidget and answered evasively, "I'm not sure which one you're talking about."

Then two men who looked like father and son came out of the back room, which appeared to be an office, and asked me what my interest in the Torah mantle was. I told them it was very important that I see it. My request must have seemed innocuous, because the men led me to the back room. One of them walked away, and the other — the older man who appeared to be the store owner — sat down behind his desk and motioned for me to have a seat.

I introduced myself, and then, as succinctly as possible, told Ann's story. When I finished, I was surprised to see the man put his face into his hands and begin to cry softly. After a few minutes, he composed himself, went out of the office, and came back carrying a large folded piece of maroon velvet. Silently, he handed it to me. I unfolded it and read the delicate Hebrew writing. My heart leaped. It was the same name Ann had given me.

I told the man it was indeed the mantle I was looking for. But before I had a chance to ask him to sell it to me, he answered, "After I acquired the mantle, I began to suspect that it might have been stolen. That's why my saleswoman was reluctant to give you any information about it. We displayed it in the window only as a sample, never thinking anyone would actually inquire about it per se.

"Now I must tell you my story. I was born in a little town in Galicia called Yaroslov. It was a beautiful life we lived. My father had a textile factory, and we were quite wealthy. In fact, we lived in a beautiful two-story brick house in the center of town. Then, one day, without warning, the tanks came in and with one blow everything was over. Finished.

"I am the only one in my entire family who survived. I went to a DP camp in Berlin after I was liberated from the concentration camp, and then after two years there, I was able to come to America. For years it tortured me that I did not have a single remembrance of my family, of my mother especially. We had been so close. But nothing was saved. Nothing was left. I didn't have so much as a piece of paper with my mother's handwriting on it."

"It kept bothering me until one day, about fifteen years ago, I decided I would go back — back to my little *shtetl* to see if anything remained. You can imagine what a trip that was. There were so many memories on every street. There were memories, but that was all. The house was gone. The factory was gone. There was not even the slightest reminder that the Fogel family had ever existed in Yaroslov.

"I realized my trip had been a waste, and I was on my way back to the hotel to pack my bags, when I passed a small photo studio owned by a gentile from the neighborhood. I looked in the window as I was passing, and there, on display, was a portrait of my mother that had been painted when she was a young bride.

"How I felt then you would not believe. Not only to find something from my childhood, but for it to be a picture of my beloved mother! I was beside myself with joy; only I quickly came back to reality. I started thinking: How should I approach the shopowner? How much should I offer? What if the owner is an anti-Semite, sees that the picture means a lot to me, and refuses to sell it? I wasn't sure how to handle the situation. In the end, I decided to tell the truth.

"I went into the shop and told the shopowner the whole story straight out. How I was originally from Yaroslov, how I now lived in America. Why I had returned and that the picture in the window was of my mother.

"The proprietor listened intently and then, without saying a word, went over to the window where the picture hung, took it down and handed it to me. My hands were shaking as I held the precious painting. I wanted to take out my wallet, but the man shook his head and pushed my hand back. He didn't want any money for the painting, he said. It belonged to me. I thanked him and left before he could change his mind. You can well imagine how much having that picture has meant to me all these years.

"After you told me the story of that poor woman, it brought back the memory of this incident. I would appreciate it if you would allow me the privilege of doing the same."

He then took out a heavy plastic bag, put the Torah mantle inside, and handed it to me.

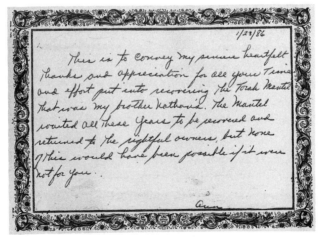

A thank-you note from Ann.

*Words that come from the heart enter the heart.*

BERACHOS 6b

The Kli Yakar asks: If words that come from the heart enter the heart, why is it that when the *Nevi'im* admonished the masses, they were not always successful?

The answer is that they "enter the heart" if there is one. If the recipient has a "heart of stone," nothing will penetrate.

# Delinquent Daughter

IN THE COURSE of my work, I am often approached by distressed and desperate parents who are having difficulty with a child. The pain and suffering they endure is of a magnitude that can't be expressed in words. These are parents who would literally give up their most precious material possessions if it could in some way bring their child back to the right path. Because of the delicate nature of this type of work, when I am asked to intervene and counsel a family, I do so with a fervent prayer that *Ha-kadosh Baruch Hu* will grant me the right words that will elicit the response I seek from the young person. Time and again I have seen how the power of speech is the most potent tool a rabbi can use to repair a broken *neshamah.* It is often the only means available with which to combat all the influences that have made a Jewish child go awry, and the way it is used spells the difference between success and failure.

O ne late spring evening last year, a distraught father called me at my office. He asked if he and his wife could meet with me to discuss their seventeen-year-old daughter. He sounded very upset and I told him to come right over. The deep lines of worry etching the faces of Mr. and Mrs. Kohen, an aristocratic-looking couple in their late forties, from a prominent Sephardic family, bespoke all they had endured the past ten months since problems with their daughter Sharon had begun.

As Mr. Kohen reached out his hand to shake mine in introduction, I saw that it trembled slightly. He began, falteringly: "Our daughter was always a perfect child. She was obedient and respectful at home. She never missed a day of school and always tried hard. She was never at the top of her class, but we didn't care. We just wanted her to do her best and follow in our ways.

"Then all of a sudden she changed. She began to speak in a chutzpadik manner to me and my wife. She began to do poorly in her religious studies. She started coming home at 2:00 or 3:00 in the morning." Here he looked away in embarrassment. "I'm ashamed to say, Rabbi, my daughter...coming home at 3:00 in the morning..."

He shook his head as if he still could not believe it. He continued, "She was associating with a wild bunch of kids. She wouldn't listen to anything we said. We tried, Rabbi, we really tried. We begged, we pleaded, we bribed. It didn't work. Nothing worked. We were really terrified. So we began to threaten her, and things just kept getting worse and worse. The more we threatened, the worse she became." He looked at me and I could see how hard it had been for him to say these things aloud.

"We are ashamed, Rabbi. We are proud people. Our

family has always been faithful to our religion and customs for generations. Now we no longer know what to do, where to turn. Please help us, Rabbi. Maybe there is still some part in her that remembers. Maybe she is still attached in some way to her mother, to her grandmother, to her great-grand-mother..." His voice trailed off. It was hard to listen to the raw anguish in this heartbroken father's voice.

I spoke encouragingly to them and asked them to bring their daughter to see me at 8:00 the next night, after I delivered a *shiur*. I assured them that I would try my best with their daughter.

Sharon arrived on time, and while her parents waited outside, she came into my office and sat down in front of my desk. She slouched low in her seat and seemed anxious to be over with whatever I was about to say. I knew this was not going to be easy.

I began speaking to Sharon. I tried to get her to say what was troubling her — what her thoughts and feelings were. No response. I reminded her of her illustrious Sephardic ancestry and how in this world we believe that those in the next world are aware of our actions. "Sharon, be a *zechus* to your ancestors. They're counting on you." Sharon looked down. She didn't answer. Her expression did not change.

I continued, "Sharon, remember the teachings of all the people who cared about you when you were a little girl. Remember the words of Torah that you have learned over the years. And, above all, Sharon, remember the precious mitzvah of *kibbud av v'em*."

Sharon remained expressionless the whole time. I could not perceive any reaction whatsoever, so I continued in this vein, adjuring her not to relinquish the privileges that were hers by virtue of the fact that she was a Jew. She appeared totally unfazed, so I tried again. "Sharon, you must realize the greatness of your *neshamah*. It has the potential to reach the highest level of spirituality in our earthly world. Don't waste it." Every ounce of conviction that I could muster, I injected into my words. She remained impassive.

After almost an hour, she abruptly stood up and said defiantly, "Look, Rabbi, I think religion is a good thing. But it's just not for me. When I get married, if I have a son, I will give him a *brit milah* and a bar mitzvah. But that's it. The rest I'm not interested in." She started to leave.

I gave it one more try. "Sharon," I called to her. She turned around. "I'd like to tell you one story, and then I will let you go." She sat down again — this time at the edge of her seat, poised to run as soon as I finished.

"There was once a great *tzaddik*, Reb Aharon Karliner. One day his disciples asked him, '*Rebbe*, what's the worst sin a Jew can commit?' Reb Aharon put his head down on the table for a long few minutes while his Chassidim waited anxiously. When he picked his head up, he answered very simply, 'My children, the worst sin a Jew can commit is to forget that he is a *ben melech*, a son of the King.' Sharon, don't you forget. Don't forget that you are a *bas melech*, that you are the daughter of the King of Kings. Don't ever forget that."

Sharon looked down at the floor for a minute. Then she left. I watched as she crossed the hall to her parents. They rushed over and hugged her. They looked inquiringly at her, their lips moving, though I could not hear what they were saying. Sharon just stared straight ahead, firmly disengaged herself from their hold, and walked right past them out the door.

I felt drained. I had given it my best, obviously without success. After a few minutes, I started turning out the lights and getting ready to leave. Suddenly Sharon burst through the door and came running back. In a trembling voice, barely able to suppress her sobs, she cried out, "*Rebbe, borcheni* — bless me!"

131

I was more than a little taken aback. I had just spoken to Sharon for close to an hour and put forth every conceivable inducement I could summon for her to reconsider her actions. I thought that I had not made even the slightest dent in her resistance — until this moment. It seems she was unable to completely disavow her upbringing, for she still believed in the potency of a *berachah* and, even more significantly, in her need for one. She still possessed the belief that a blessing would in some way protect and perhaps ultimately redeem her.

I knew this would probably be my one last chance with Sharon. Hopefully, the words I would choose would be auspicious ones. I blessed her: "Sharon, may you be *zocheh* to realize the value of the soul that is within you. May you be *zocheh* to be a source of *nachas* to your parents, grandparents, and great-grandparents. And may you have *hatzlachah* always in all the good things you do." Crying bitterly, she thanked me for the *berachah* and ran back outside to her parents.

Mr. Kohen called the next day. He said that Sharon had cried for a long time when they got home. "We left her alone. When she stopped crying she came into our room and told us she would try. Rabbi, that's all we can ask of her at this point." And I agreed.

Within the next few weeks, the Kohens kept me apprised of Sharon's progress. Slowly she had begun to resume a lifestyle acceptable for a true Jewish daughter.

*The years of a person's life are seventy...*

TEHILLIM 90

The Belzer Rebbe explained that the seventy years mentioned in the *pasuk* are related to the seven years between bar mitzvah and age twenty for a boy, and ages twelve and nineteen for a girl. He felt that these seven years were the most significant ones in the character development of a human being and also correspond to the seventy years which constitute a person's natural lifetime. This means that we must be especially careful during our children's teenage years to teach them the right *hashkafos* and provide a positive Torah environment because this will shape and mold their entire outlook on life.

# The Shabbos Siren

I have always been interested in and acutely aware of the vast resources that lie within the souls, minds, and hearts of our young people. The potential for using these precious resources to a *neshamah*'s best advantage has always been a challenge for me.

So it was with alacrity and enthusiasm that I accepted a position as *manhig ruchani* (religious adviser) at a Jewish Federation camp in the foothills of Virginia.

For one thing, the *gashmiyus* — the camp and the campsite — were spectacular. In fact, I would not doubt that the words bucolic, picturesque, and scenic were coined specifically to describe it. It was filled with rolling green hills, immaculately manicured lawns, and startlingly clear blue skies, all brought out to their best advantage by the awesome mountainous backdrop. The four hundred campers were mostly from affluent Jewish homes in the Philadelphia and Virginia area, and judging by the looks of the bunkhouses, which were remarkably reminiscent of Swiss chalets, one could easily tell that these kids were not there to rough it.

My job, as the only rabbi on campgrounds, was to introduce and provide spirituality and proper *hashkafos* for the older groups. Although there were a few challenges, the job could not have been easier. These young people were phenomenally receptive. Their thirst for Torah knowledge and halachic practices was unquenchable and their absorption of *divrei Torah* and *mussar* was extraordinary. We had many discussions which ranged from the Torah viewpoint on euthanasia, the sources that prove there really is life after death, to what relevance Shabbos has in today's world. Together we tackled them all. They questioned, I answered. They reacted with wide-eyed wonderment and fascination with the marvelous intricacies and beauty of their heritage. In truth, it was uplifting for me as well, and I enjoyed our sessions immensely.

As Rav, I was permitted free rein, and I tried to reach out to just about everyone in camp — campers, counselors, right up to the camp director. In this capacity, I met a couple of Israeli *shelichim*, Uri and Tova. These two had been sent to the camp by the Israeli government to try to inculcate American Jewish youth with a love for Israel and perhaps convince them to spend some time working on a *kibbutz*. Needless to say, the rigors of *kibbutz* life did not appeal that much to these campers. But Tova and Uri were not daunted. They were articulate, self-confident, and highly intelligent young people. They were also, unfortunately, totally devoid of religious training and background.

I tried to make a connection with them by drawing them into conversations about their Jewishness. It's difficult to say how much was accomplished with Tova. She was good-natured, but I could not pin her down to any earnest discussion. With Uri, however, I felt that at least he showed some interest in many different issues from a Torah perspective. Why couldn't a person pray in his own words? What's a messiah? It was as if Uri were just doing some religious browsing, glancing curiously at this and that, yet not really ready to actually buy anything at all.

Once, I decided to arrange a special Friday night Shabbos *seudah* for the staff only. I was really excited at the prospect of being able to offer these kids a traditional Shabbos meal, and I suppose my enthusiasm was contagious because most of the counselors accepted my invitation eagerly. I took pains with the preparation of the meal and knew as I surveyed the table and recited *Kiddush* that Friday night that it really showed. In the center of the table, on a small tray I had borrowed from the kitchen staff, were the two lit Shabbos candles. The candles suffused everything on the table and the faces of those seated around it with that special light that only one who has experienced a Shabbos can really know, and the meal went better than I had hoped.

We sang *zemiros* and we talked. They listened avidly to the *divrei Torah* on the *parashah*, and I could tell that everyone was enjoying himself. Unfortunately, I did not see Tova or Uri. When I asked one of the others where they were, they seemed a little embarrassed and murmured something about "evening off"..."in town"..."couldn't make it".... I was a little disappointed they had not come, but I didn't allow it to spoil my *oneg Shabbos*.

After we *bentch*ed together, everyone said *gut Shabbos* and left when the lights in the dining room went out. I decided to stay and read a *sefer* by the light of the candles. The evening was still with that complete kind of stillness one feels only in the country, and although there was not a single disturbing noise, I did not hear Uri walk into the dining room. Rather, I sensed someone's presence across the table. I looked up and was startled to see him standing there, staring silently at the two dwindling Shabbos *licht*. His eyes were glistening brightly, but I wasn't certain if it was the reflection of the candles or tears. Uri looked as if he were in a trance, as if he were seeing something much more than just two small Shabbos candles.

He noticed me watching him and gave an almost guilty little jump, as if he had been doing something wrong.

"Is it okay for me to look at the candles, Rabbi?" he asked.

I assured him that of course it was.

Then he began speaking as if we had been in the middle of a conversation. "I was about eight years old. We went to Givat Shaul, a neighborhood in Yerushalayim, to visit my grandmother. She was my mother's mother. It was Friday afternoon and I was really excited. I loved my grandmother. She was exactly what any little boy's dream of a grandmother would be. She was warm, with those nice crinkly lines alongside her eyes that made you think she was smiling, even when she wasn't. I was her only grandchild. My mother was her only child. My *savta* had lived through the camps. My grandfather had died the year before and I guess I was pretty precious to her. But we didn't visit her too often because she was *dati* (religious), and my mother thought that stuff was old-fashioned and outdated. She didn't feel she had much in common with her mother anymore, so we kept our distance, although we did go visit her now and then.

"That Friday, we got to my *savta*'s house just as the sirens signaling the beginning of Shabbat were sounding. I always loved the sound of that siren. It made it seem like Shabbat was such a big deal — its arrival was announced so loudly and so importantly. Funny, I used to wonder sometimes what you were supposed to do on Shabbat. I was only eight, but I used to wonder. *Savta* had already lit her Shabbat candles and I could see her lips moving silently. Finally she uncovered her eyes and looked straight at me in such a peculiar way that I knew without question that her whispered prayer had been about me. All she said, though, was, '*Shabbat Shalom.*'

"We stayed that Friday evening with my *savta* and drove home later on. I don't think we ever visited my grandmother again on Shabbat, because this is the first time that I've seen lit Shabbat candles since that one time in her house.''

"Uri," I asked, "what happened to your *savta?*"

"Oh, she died a few years ago, and you know what, I miss her." He turned around quickly and with a *"Shabbat shalom"* hurried out of the dining room.

Uri's second encounter with the intrinsic *kedushah* of Shabbos, epitomized by the lit Shabbos candles, proved to be the turning point in his life. He started coming to *shiurim* and paying close attention to what I said. His questions became more specific, and he asked to delve more and more deeply into the concrete subject matter that would enable him to live his life as an Observant Jew. By the time the summer was over, I felt that Uri had advanced considerably along precisely that path.

*Epilogue:*

A few years later, I received a letter from Uri. He was attending a yeshiva in Yerushalayim and wanted me to know that when he married, he would be certain that his wife, like his *savta,* would light Shabbat candles and share with him a Torah-true life. I am sure the light of those candles will shine straight through to *Gan Eden* and give his *savta* much *nachas.*

When an unidentified body is found on the road between two cities, the citizens of each city must come together and say, "Our hands did not spill this blood. It was not because we allowed this traveler to leave our city unaccompanied that he died." From this we learn how important it is to accompany a Jew on his way.

# Room 1349

It was about 4:00 in the afternoon on a very hot Friday in August. I was the *manhig ruchani* of a large Jewish Federation overnight camp in the foothills of Virginia, and the summer had thus far been a peaceful one. But on that particular day, as I sat under a tree learning *parashas Shoftim*, I noticed a crowd of counselors and campers in the distance, gathered in a small, noisy knot. I quickly walked over to them to find out what the commotion was all about, and saw that the nurse and head counselor were kneeling on the ground next to an eleven-year-old camper who was clutching his knee in obvious pain. They told me the boy had fallen and the nurse suspected that his leg might be broken.

They were waiting for a car to take the boy to the hospital for X-rays. It was only a few hours before Shabbos and it seemed that only the camp driver was available to accompany him. Wishing to reassure the frightened and hurt camper, I climbed into the back seat along with him.

At the hospital, there was a two-hour wait to be X-rayed. My camper was resting comfortably in a special waiting area for patients only, where I was not permitted to enter. I decided to take a look at the clergy registry and visit some of the Jewish patients while I was waiting. There were five Jewish names on the list. I chose to visit the patient whose room was on the thirteenth floor, because I assumed he probably had the fewest number of visitors since his room was so far away from the main entrance. When I came out of the elevator, I saw the corridor was entirely deserted and eerily quiet. Even the lights in the hall seemed dimmer than downstairs. There was none of the hustle and bustle of a hospital. There were no nurses, no phones ringing, no activity. Only a sepulchral stillness.

The room I was looking for was all the way at the other end. I walked to room 1349, my footsteps echoing loudly. The door was closed. I knocked, but no one answered. I knocked again, but still no one answered, although I heard someone moving around inside. I decided to open the door and go in. Perhaps the man was too ill or feeble to speak or call out.

At the sound of my entrance, the patient, who had been lying on his side with his back to the door, spun around. He was startled to see me. I, in turn, was saddened to see him. Alexander was a young man of about eighteen, who seemed to be only a shadow of the health one might expect for his age. His skin was pallid and gray — he must have been confined to the hospital for quite a while. I sat down on the chair next to his bed, feeling a strong sense of compassion for this young person.

Alex immediately began to question me in a suspicious, almost belligerent manner. Who was I and what did I want? I explained I was a rabbi. I had seen his name in the clergy registry and had come to see how he was feeling. He continued to question me. Who sent you? Was it my mother? Was it the hospital? Was it the social services agency? Why are you here? I again explained patiently, trying to speak soothingly, for he seemed very agitated.

141

"Alex, no one sent me. I came only to visit a fellow Jew. I saw your name, I knew you were Jewish, so I came up to visit you. My being here is as simple as that." Alex put his head in his hands and began crying bitterly, all the while saying, "Nobody sent you. Nobody sent you." After two minutes he stopped crying and said, "It was very nice of you to come and see me, a stranger. It was nice." He seemed to relax a bit.

I asked him, "Alex, tell me why you are here." He began to answer in half-sentences. Haltingly, and bit by bit, his tragic history unfolded. As he spoke, almost as if against his will, years of pent-up thoughts and emotions began pouring out in a torrent.

"I've been here for three months. I'm not really sick, you know. Though I guess you could say I am — I'm sick in the head, I'm sick in my heart, and I'm sick of everything." He stopped for a moment. "I'm here three months...three months. Do you know why, Rabbi? Not for the usual reasons. Only..." he paused again, as if he could not bear to say it, "I am...was...a drug addict. A drug addict," he said it again bitterly. "Now I'm clean, but who knows?

"I started doing drugs when I was only fourteen. For no reason. I had a regular childhood, but a lot of the other kids were doing it. I was curious and I wanted to try it. Then you know what happens. I tried it once, twice, three times. I was hooked. I began to act weird. I lied; I stole. It took quite a while for my parents to catch on. In the beginning they had no idea why I was acting so crazy. They tried talking to me, to my teachers, to the school counselors. Nothing helped. I just kept on doing things my way. I couldn't stop.

"After a while, my parents found out. They tried to help me. I admit it. They tried to help me. But I didn't want to be helped. I just wouldn't stop. I couldn't stop. I left home when I was sixteen and roamed the streets. It's an awful story; you've probably heard it before, Rabbi. When even I couldn't stand myself anymore, I came to the rehabilitation center — the detox program in this hospital.

"While I was on the street I kept in touch with my parents from time to time. I would call them, mostly to ask for money. Then I told them I was in the hospital. But in all these months they haven't once come to see me. I let them know I was being released soon. You know what they told me? They said, 'Don't bother coming home. Your stuff is out on the street.'" He began to cry again, hard and uncontrollably. "I don't blame them."

"I have no place to go from here. Who knows where I'll be three months from now? Probably right back where I was before. Sometimes I think I should just...you know...kill myself. I think it would be best for everyone. I'm scared, Rabbi. I've gotta tell you, I'm really scared. I don't want to go back to the way I was. I want to change. I want to turn my life around, but I don't know how. I don't know where to start. You're the first person who ever showed he cared about me, not because he had to because I was his patient or kid or something, but simply because I was a human being." Alex stopped talking, and I thought he had finished. Then he added, "And a Jew. You'll never know how much I appreciate that."

At that moment, the words of the Rashi I had been learning a little while earlier sprang to mind: "Our hands did not spill this blood." Unfortunately, no one would accompany Alex. He would leave the hospital all alone, with no one to help him along the difficult road ahead, and the consequences would be on *klal Yisrael*'s head.

I spoke to Alex as much as time would allow, encouraging him and offering him hope. I told him, "Alex, you do have a purpose in life. You do have someone who cares about you. You are a Jew and you have thousands of years behind you, backing you up. You have your heritage, you have your birthright, and most importantly, you have Hashem, Who loves each and every one of His children and cares deeply about each one."

We spoke a while longer. Finally, I wished Alex a good Shabbos. He asked very tentatively, "Rabbi, will you come again?" I gave him many assurances that of course I would and then went downstairs to see my camper who had just come out of X-ray. His leg was fortunately not broken.

On the way back to camp, I thought about sending something to Alex with the driver. Alex had mentioned he was an artist, and I had remembered seeing a beautiful art book in the camp library containing photographs of wooden synagogues. I put the book in a bag along with two challos, a few slices of fish, and some cake and sent it off.

That Shabbos I could not stop thinking about Alex's situation. I kept thinking about this floundering *neshamah*, desperate to be rescued. He was a Jew who felt so alone in the world, yet was unaware of how close his solace actually was.

That *motza'ei Shabbos*, as soon as I made *havdalah* for the camp, I returned to the hospital and spoke with Alex a long while.

The day before Alex was to be released, I came to the hospital for what had become, over the past two weeks, my daily visit. I found him out of bed and pacing his room impatiently. I marveled at how improved his appearance was compared to the first time I had seen him. Part of it was that he now had some color. But most importantly, when I looked at him, I saw a certain measure of serenity, even a bit of self-confidence, that had not been there before. Alex came over when he saw me and excitedly shook my hand. We sat down to talk. I knew this would be our last meeting, and I felt a pang of helplessness, wondering how Alex would react to being back on the street. We spoke a while — about life, about *emunah*, and about Alex. Then it was time for me to leave. I stood up, gave Alex a *berachah*, and wished him continued *hatzlachah* as he made his way down the long path to complete recovery. I hoped that at least my words of *chizuk* and my sincerest wishes for his success would accompany him and protect him from harm.

Just as I was about to leave, Alex jumped up from his chair and said, "Rabbi, wait!" I stopped. "I've been thinking. I've really been thinking. All my life I looked for something, some crutch to help me through. I needed outside things to make me feel good. Until now it was drugs." He gave a bitter laugh. "Yeah, I felt good, but it only lasted for a little while. Rabbi, tell me the truth. Do you think they would take me?"

I didn't realize to whom Alex was referring. "Who, Alex? Do I think who would take you?"

"Do you think that yeshiva you mentioned for guys like me — I don't know the first thing about Judaism, I mean I didn't even have a bar mitzvah — do you think they would accept me?"

Alex was looking at me intently. It was the first glimmer of hope I had seen emanate from him in all the time I had known him.

I said reassuringly and emphatically, "Alex I don't *think* they will take you, I *know* they will."

In *Bava Metzia* 21b, the law of unconscious abandonment (*ye'ush she'lo mi-da'as*) is an interesting one. Abaye maintains that if one despairs of retrieving a lost article, it is not considered as if he has legally abandoned it.

The Kotzker says in a poignant observation: If a man comes to a state of despair (*ye'ush*), it is only through lack of knowledge (*she'lo mi-da'as*). Despair stems from ignorance.

# *Lost and Found*

"I've come to the end of the line, Rabbi. You're my last chance."

How many times have I heard those words uttered out of fear, out of hopelessness, out of desperation! For a rabbi, it is a heavy but sanctified burden to know that another *Yid* had placed his future success, happiness, or good fortune in his hands.

I look back on problems brought to me that appeared to be without conceivable resolution, and I see the *siyatta di-Shmaya* that effects the solution.

Phyllis admitted, as she sat on the other side of my desk, that she had already exhausted every possibility. She had hired a private detective and even consulted astrologers, all to no avail. Out of desperation, she had gone to see another rabbi who, when he heard what her problem was, had replied, "I'm sorry, but since you're not a congregant at my shul, I can't become involved."

147

Not surprisingly, therefore, she said, "I've come to the end of the line, Rabbi. You're my last chance." Those were her first words to me.

Indeed Phyllis' problem was complex: "Ten years ago I got divorced. It's not really important to go into all the sordid details, Rabbi. But the bottom line is that it was all for the best. As soon as everything was finalized, I packed my bags and left my hometown. I wanted to get away from everything that reminded me of the bad times. I looked for a new apartment and a new job. I wanted to start over again. Everything would have been fine, except for one thing — my son."

"You see, Rabbi, he was nineteen at the time. The divorce hit him hard. He didn't really know whose side he was on. One morning, right before I got my divorce papers, I found a note on the kitchen table when I came down for breakfast."

Phyllis pulled a small piece of paper out of her pocket and carefully unfolded it. There were sharp creases where the note had obviously been unfolded and refolded many times. She handed it to me, and I read, "I'm leaving. I don't know if I will ever see you again. Doug."

"I haven't seen or heard from him since," Phyllis said.

I expressed my sympathy to Phyllis and asked how I could help her.

She looked hesitant. "Rabbi, I need to ask you for something and you may think it's crazy. I want you to help me find my son."

I didn't know how to respond. How could I help her find a grown-up son whom she had not seen in ten years: whom she had not heard from or had any contact with and who had deliberately severed connections?

Then, as if sensing my loss for words, she repeated her plea, "You see, I'm getting older. I must go in for surgery — I need an operation on my eyes. I've been putting it off for a while, but I can't wait much longer. I am losing my vision. I want my son there when they operate. I need him. I've got to find him. Will you help me?''

After a moment's contemplation, I said, "Phyllis, there's a special prayer a Jew says when he finds himself in a troubled state. It's from the Book of Psalms." I gave her a *Tehillim* with an English translation and told her to say Chapter 22 every day. "In addition, there is a special *segulah*, a sort of talisman, for finding something that's lost. Try it."

"Yes, Rabbi, what is it?"

"Put a small amount of charity into a special charity box," I explained, "and say the words, '*Elokah d'Rav Meir Aneni*.' These few words have been known to have tremendous power when a person has given up all hope of finding something lost."

I could see Phyllis's face changing expression from despair to hope. "I'll do it, Rabbi," she said. "I'll say the psalms every day and I'll give charity. I pray it will work."

"If you have faith — *bitachon*, Phyllis — I'm sure it will," I encouraged her.

A month passed. Phyllis had still not been able to find Doug, although she recited psalms and gave the charity faithfully every day.

A short while later, an invitation arrived for her to attend an ecological conference in Vermont. Since ecology was a strong and abiding interest of hers, she made plans to attend.

At the conference, Phyllis enjoyed the seminars and the workshops, never for one minute forgetting what had become an all-consuming pain in her heart. On the last evening of her stay, Phyllis's bags were packed for her early morning flight. She sat in the large cafeteria with a cup of coffee in front of her and gloomily looked through the large plate glass windows as the last bit of daylight disappeared.

Suddenly she jumped up and ran outside onto the grounds she had been half-heartedly observing from inside the cafeteria. She ran faster and faster. There in front of her, only a few feet away, walked a young man.

"Doug," she called, at first softly and tentatively, then louder and stronger, "Doug!"

The young man whirled around and stopped when he saw the middle-aged woman running towards him.

Phyllis ran up to him, stopped, and just stood looking at her son. "Doug," she was trying to catch her breath. "I found you at last." Then she hugged him tightly and began to cry. "My boy...Doug, I want to make it up to you. Please, Doug, give me a chance."

He was pulling away from her. His face registered only shocked surprise. "Mother, I don't know how you found me. I will have to take time to get used to this. I can't believe this. How did you find me? How?" he kept repeating.

"Doug, it's a long story. It wasn't easy. All it took was a little faith."

"Please." He tried to pull away. "I need some time to get used to this."

"Please, Doug, can I call you?" Phyllis asked.

"No, not yet. I think we should only write. Write me a letter. Here's my address, and I'll write back. I'm sorry. I just never expected this to happen. I have to get used to it. Please understand. I thought we would never see each other again. It will take time."

"Okay, Doug, whatever you say."

They exchanged addresses and reluctantly, afraid she might lose him again, Phyllis said goodbye. They corresponded with each other for a few months. Then Phyllis could no longer delay her operation. She wrote to Doug that she would be going into the hospital and left it at that.

After her recuperation, Phyllis came to my office and told me, "When I was wheeled out of surgery, the first person I saw was my son."

# *Kumarov Vignettes*

FOR MOST JEWS, Poland immediately evokes multiple and conflicting images. Our parents and grandparents recall it as though it had been the paradigm of Jewish life. They remember the pure *neshamos* who lived there: the water carrier, the butcher, the *shochet*, the *shammash*. They remember with complete clarity the holy *tzaddikim* they had the *zechus* of knowing, whose counsel they were once privileged to seek, whose words of Torah they were once able to hear. They remember walking to shul on Friday night with friends, family, and neighbors, and they cry when they remember.

They also remember the dreadful poverty: staying indoors during the winter for lack of a pair of shoes, the unremitting hunger, and the bare, cold one-room houses. They remember the Polish peasants, the fear of unprovoked attacks, and the senseless, vicious pogroms. They remember it all, and they cry when they remember

*Olam she'hayah v'ennenu*
A world that was and is no longer...

151

left: *Kever* of the
Vorki Rebbe *ztz"l*.
below: *Kevarim* of the
Brisker Rav (r.) and the
Netziv (l.) in Warsaw.

*At the giving of the Torah, with every word that emanated from the mouth of* Ha-kadosh Baruch Hu, *each Jew's* neshamah *left him. Hashem then took out the special dew that in the future will revive the dead, and He revived them.*

SHABBOS 88b

The *Sefas Emes* asks why was it necessary for the Jewish People to endure this trauma? First their *neshamos* expired, and then they were brought back from the dead. He answers that this showed every Jew for all eternity that in order to accept the Torah completely, one must do so with *mesiras nefesh* — self-sacrifice.

# Visas and Vistas

few years ago, the Lauder Foundation invited me to Poland to act as rabbi in a summer camp for Jewish adults. That I would be able to actualize something that had heretofore only been an illusory image, that I would be able to tread the same paths my forefathers had walked, that I would be *zocheh* to visit the *tzaddikim* in the *beis ha-kevaros* of Ger, Radomsk, Piliver, Volozhin, Brisk, Kotsk...Vurke... that my *zeides* had seen in life was to realize what had been until then only an evanescent wishfulness.

That was how I came to be standing in the Warsaw airport, surrounded by hundreds of Poles arriving from various flights. I knew there would be a long wait until I cleared customs, so I took out a *sefer* and became engrossed in my learning. Suddenly, I began to feel extremely conspicuous, as though there were hundreds of eyes looking at me. When I picked up my head, I saw that, indeed, it was a fact. Everyone in the busy airport had stopped and turned in my direction to stare at me. For a second, I could not understand what was so interesting. Then I realized that for these people, seeing a Jew dressed as a Jew and acting as a Jew was so anomalous and unusual that it had caused them to come to a standstill. It was as if a species they had thought was extinct had suddenly come to life. This was my chilling introduction to Poland.

A car and driver were waiting outside the airport for us, and as we drove through the streets of Warsaw, it was surprising how many buildings and streets in the city seemed to have remained intact from before the war. The narrow dirt roads, the attached, crowded buildings, and the dark and dank alleyways all served to intensify the feeling of having been transported back in time. Even the people looked as poverty-stricken and hungry as they must have looked fifty years ago. It seemed like Poland had not really changed very much over the years.

The camp was located in a suburb of Warsaw called Kumarov. There were about fifty adults there who participated in the activities, and they ranged in age from about fifteen to seventy. When we arrived, we were shown to our accommodations, and after refreshing ourselves, we were asked to join everyone for the evening meal. The dining room was already filled when we entered, and after I had washed and eaten a piece of bread, I was served a bowl of soup. I ate the soup at a normal pace and after a few minutes was finished. I noticed, however, that everyone else in the room was still eating his soup. I waited and waited for everyone to finish, but they continued to eat their soup for what seemed like an inordinately long time. When finally everyone had finished, we *bentch*ed. The bowl of soup had been the entire meal. Such was the scarcity of food...

The first Shabbos in camp was also the first real Shabbos that many of these Jews had ever experienced, and they seemed to relish every moment of it as well as every nuance of the laws and customs. *Licht-bentchen, Kiddush,* challah, the meal, the singing — everything generated enthusiastic excitement in our "campers." Friday night, when I was giving everyone a piece of challah after *Ha-motzi*, I noticed one woman in her late sixties eating her piece while tears streamed down her face. I went over and asked her, "Yasha, why are you crying?"

Immediately she answered, "I am crying for the Shabbos. This is the first time I have tasted challah since before the War. Now I am crying for all the many Shabbosos that have passed since then that are forever lost to me...all those many Shabbosos that I did not eat challah. I can never regain those times."

From time to time Jews from around the world who had come to Poland to visit the cemeteries where their ancestors were buried would come to the camp to observe and even sometimes participate in the activities. One was a middle-aged man, around fifty-five, from Eretz Yisrael. Boruch Segal had been born in Poland and, in fact, had lived not that far from where the camp was. He told me that he knew many of the "campers" and their families from before the War. Then he related to me the following story:

"The Nazis had lined us all up to be deported to Buchenwald. One woman, a neighbor of ours, was holding her daughter, who was a tiny infant, in her arms. As we stood there, the woman who was barely religious and certainly not in any way Chassidic, noticed that down the line — also waiting to be deported — was the holy *tzaddik* from Alexander. She left the line, which in itself could have meant an instant death sentence, and ran over to the *rebbe.* She proceeded to implore him to bless her child that she should survive the war. The *rebbe* turned kindly to her — I was standing close by and overheard every word he said — and blessed her: 'May your daughter live a long life and may she one day become a leader of her community.'

"I could see the relief in that woman's eyes. It was as though she were sure that in the face of whatever might happen, the *berachah* from the *tzaddik* would be fulfilled and she need no longer worry about her child's welfare. So strong was her simple faith..."

Then Boruch turned to me with a smile and, pointing openly to a woman in her forties who was the leader of a group that had come to the camp from Vilna, he declared, "*She* was that baby."

During our stay in Poland we had the privilege of *davening* at the holy *beis ha-kevaros* of Reb Chaim of Brisk, Reb Shimon Sofer, the Tosafos Yom Tov, the Megaleh Amukos, the Divrei Shmuel of Slonim, and the Me'or Ve-shemesh.

We visited the shul where the Rema had once been the Rav. There the Rema's chair, which has been kept in perfect condition for hundreds of years, stands, although a large piece of wood has been nailed across the arms to prevent anyone from sitting in it. Quite interestingly, the *shammash* of the shul is a woman in her sixties, who faithfully preserves and protects the premises...

We stood at the site of what had once been the Warsaw ghetto and for some reason I wondered how the *Yidden* had felt at their last Pesach Seder, when they said the words, "*L'shanah ha-ba'ah bi-Yerushalayim.*"

Our last stop, and I suppose it could be termed the nadir of our visit to Poland, was a visit to Auschwitz. I went with about six people who had requested that I recite *Kel malei rachamim* for their parents who had perished in the camps. What can be said that has not already been said an infinite number of times in an infinite number of ways about standing on the blood-soaked earth of Auschwitz? The roiling emotions that washed through me simply from standing in the same spot

My summer as rabbi at a summer camp
for Jewish adults in Kumarov, Poland.

Auschwitz.

where countless innocent *neshamos* once stood before going to their unspeakable and unimaginable deaths, simply defies expression. But, to add even more horror to the place's heinous aura was how Auschwitz had become a bona fide tourist attraction, complete with a mini-bazaar in the parking lot, where vendors hawked everything from sunglasses and T-shirts to slides of Auschwitz, and where casually clad tourists from all over snapped pictures of one another against this or that background.

My group and I walked along the path that led through the camp. We passed the unloading area where Jews were herded off the cattle cars, the selection area, and the barracks. None of us were able to utter a single word. Finally we came to the gas chambers. I felt this was the proper place to stop and say the *Kel malei rachamim.* I took out my *siddur,* and as my group stood nearby, I intoned the prayer for the holy martyrs who gave their lives *al kiddush Hashem.* I had never said it before in such a state of brokenheartedness.

At the time, I did not notice that a group of non-Jews from Stockholm had stopped nearby. They were standing still, listening to my words of prayer with their heads bowed respectfully. When I finished, I saw that everyone in my group was crying bitterly. Surprisingly, I also noticed that the members of the group from Stockholm, who did not understand a word of Hebrew, were crying too...

Last minute arrangements and preparations for our departure from Poland kept us quite busy. But before we left, the whole group with whom we had spent the past three weeks gathered in the lecture hall for one last talk. As I spoke, I noticed two young men in front of me passing a note. The recipient of the note read it, nodded sadly, and I could see tears fill his eyes. When I finished speaking, I was curious about what had been written in the note. I asked the young man who had written it to show it to me. Opening the small, white folded paper, I saw the words, "Next Shabbos who will make *Kiddush* for us?"

As we were saying our goodbyes, one tall young man, about seventeen years old, named Mathieusz came over and asked if he could speak to me alone for a few minutes. We went into a small room where we would have some privacy. As soon as we got inside, Mathieusz closed the door and opened his shirt. I saw he was wearing a pair of *tzitzis* so small it would have fit a three-year-old. He pulled out one of the *tzitzis*, which was frayed, to show me, and asked, "Rabbi, are my *tzitzis* kosher?"

Tears came to my eyes from the simple humility of his question. Here was this devoted young man living in a country where it was nothing less than a miracle that he had remained a Jew, let alone a Jew that observed mitzvos, who regarded the mitzvah of wearing *tzitzis* so highly that he was wearing the only pair he could acquire — those of a small child...and was concerned about whether or not they were kosher! I quickly removed the pair of *tzitzis* I was wearing and handed it to him. "Mathieusz," I said, "wear this — I know it is kosher."

Many of the group we had taught accompanied us to the airport to see us off. We were saying a final farewell when I noticed that Basha, a young girl of about eighteen, was standing on the side by herself and crying bitterly. I went over and inquired as to why she was so upset.

"I participated in many student protests and demonstrations," she said, "and because of it the government has taken away my passport. Now I can never get a visa to leave this place." She looked through the large window longingly at the plane that was waiting to take us back to America.

"I want to leave. This is no place for a Jew to live, only to die," she said almost angrily. I felt so saddened by the desolation and despair in Basha's words. I tried to think of something to say that would encourage her. Then I told her, "Someday soon, Basha, *Mashiach* will come, and I promise you he will come with Basha's visa in his hand." She tried to smile but was not very successful.

As I started to walk to my plane, I glanced back at the sorrowful faces of those we were leaving behind, and reflected in them I saw the 2,000 years of *golus* we have all endured. That was when I realized that my blessing to Basha applied to us all.

*Though my father and mother have forsaken me, Hashem will gather me in....*

TEHILLIM 27:10

# *Homeless*

I had just finished *daven*ing and was putting away my *tallis* and *tefillin,* when Benny burst through the door of the shul and came rushing over.

"Rabbi, I need your help." He spoke breathlessly, as if he had run a great distance.

I saw that he was extremely agitated. "Calm down, Benny. What's the problem?"

"Rabbi, it's my cousin. He passed away last night. His parents aren't religious. They know he should probably have a Jewish burial, but they don't care either way. I want him to have one, Rabbi. You see, we were the same age. At one time we were close. What should I do, Rabbi? Will you take care of it?"

I assured him that I would, and then Benny seemed to calm down. "Okay, I'll tell them, Rabbi. I'll tell them he'll have a Jewish burial." He wiped away his tears. "The poor guy."

"Benny, do you want to talk about it? I know it's hard ..."

"You see, Rabbi, Sandy — my cousin — he was only thirty,

163

but as far as he was concerned— as far as we all were concerned — he had died a long time ago. He was always a very
sensitive guy. Even when we were growing up, he would take
everything to heart, more than anybody else. My family is
Sephardic, but unfortunately not very religious. We observe a
lot of customs, but not much more.

"My aunt and uncle, Sandy's parents, probably had the
least to do with religion than anyone else in the family. Sandy
grew up barely knowing he was a Jew. His parents sent him to
the best schools, to the best college. He got a job working in
a brokerage firm when he graduated. He started at the bottom
as some kind of clerk, but he was going up, getting promo-
tions, raises.

"Then, the stock market crashed. He was laid off. I guess
you could say that was it for him. He tried to find another job,
but, you know, there were a lot of people looking for the same
kind of job.

"He finally gave up...sat at home, read the newspaper or
slept, and didn't do much of anything. Sometimes my aunt
heard him in his room talking to himself. He would just talk
and talk. Then he began acting strange in other ways. He
would stare straight in front of him for hours. Then he started
wandering the streets. All day he just walked around aimlessly.

"His parents begged him to get help, but he refused. He
wandered all day, and then one night he just didn't come
home at all. His parents were frantic. They went searching for
him and found him sleeping in a doorway. When they woke
him, he wouldn't come home with them.

"He began living on the streets. He became one of the
homeless. The only thing was, Sandy had a home. He just
refused to go to it. His parents asked the cop who patrolled
the area where Sandy slept to keep an eye on him. Day by day,
week by week, poor Sandy just deteriorated. He was filthy. He
muttered to himself. He asked people for money and some-

times they gave him. I guess that's how he survived as long as he did. His parents tried; we all begged him: 'Sandy, come home. We love you. We care about you. Come back home.' But he wouldn't listen. He couldn't listen. The poor guy.

"Then we just gave up on him. We didn't hear anything from Sandy for about a year. Last night, the cop called my aunt and uncle. He was patrolling his beat when he saw Sandy lying in a doorway. He walked over and called to him, but Sandy didn't answer or move. When the cop leaned over, he realized Sandy was dead."

What I heard was shocking and tragic. What a waste of a human life, I thought. What a waste of a *Yiddishe neshamah*.

"Like I told you, Rabbi, my aunt and uncle are not religious at all. They don't want to have anything to do with this whole mess. They're angry at Sandy. They feel he should have done more or something...who knows? They couldn't really accept that he had gotten sick."

I expressed my sympathy to Benny and gave him a few words of *chizuk*. "The *Ribbono shel Olam* takes care of every *neshamah*, Benny. Your cousin's is now in His hands. You don't have to worry about him anymore." I told Benny whom to call for the funeral arrangements.

Throughout the rest of the day I kept thinking about Benny's cousin. How proficient a city dweller becomes in learning to step around and avert his gaze from the homeless who are blocking sidewalks and doorways. How could one imagine that one of those unfortunate souls actually has a mother, father, relatives, a home? Who could imagine they would choose to deliberately sleep and live, instead, in the street?

I was very disturbed by these thoughts. How did this happen and why?

That night I went to bed a little earlier than usual. I tossed and turned for hours, waking up and falling back asleep.

Toward morning, however, I fell into a deep sleep and had a very vivid dream.

I was in what seemed to be a Middle Eastern country. I was *daven*ing before the *amud* in a brightly lit shul. As I reached *Kerias Shema*, I suddenly realized that there were three men standing around me. They were dressed in Sephardic attire — with large, embroidered skullcaps and long ornate robes. Their faces radiated holiness. I stopped *daven*ing and looked up at them inquiringly.

They asked in Hebrew, "Who will say *Kaddish* for the *neshamah* of Shaul ben Yaakov?" Then they repeated three times. "Who will say *Kaddish* for Shaul ben Yaakov?"

I woke up and felt very disturbed by the dream. It had been so strange. I felt I was being asked to do something. I was not sure what.

After *daven*ing that morning, Benny came into the shul. We would be going to his cousin's funeral together. Benny looked downcast. "Poor Sandy; poor guy," he kept repeating.

"Benny," I asked him, "what was your cousin Sandy's Hebrew name?"

"His Hebrew name?" Benny asked, perplexed. "Sandy is a Jewish name."

"No, what was his given name, the name he received at his *bris*?"

"Rabbi, I don't know. Everyone always called him Sandy."

"Who would know, Benny? It's very important."

"I guess his parents know. We could ask them when we get to the funeral."

We drove the short distance to the funeral home. As soon as we walked in, Benny went right over to his uncle, who was just sitting on a bench, staring straight ahead. He seemed almost angry to be there. "Uncle Joey, what was Sandy's Hebrew name?"

His uncle looked up. "His Hebrew name? We never used it. What's the difference what it was?"

"C'mon, Uncle Joey. The rabbi needs to know."

"The rabbi?" He glanced in my direction. "Okay. We named him Shaul at his *bris milah*, but we never called him that."

"Okay, okay. And what's yours, Uncle Joey? What's your Hebrew name?"

"Mine? What do you need that for? The tombstone? We can order that later..."

"No, Uncle Joey. The rabbi needs to know your Hebrew name too. What is it?"

Seeing how insistent Benny was, his uncle answered, exasperated, "It's Yaakov. Don't you remember when you were a little boy Grandpa used to..."

As Benny and his uncle talked, my dream returned to me again in all its clarity.

Who will say *Kaddish* for Shaul ben Yaakov? I had been *zocheh* to witness an application of the *pasuk*, "Though my father and mother forsake me, God will still gather me unto Him." For eleven months after his death, I deemed it a Divine obligation to say *Kaddish* for the *neshamah* of Shaul ben Yaakov.

*May Hashem deliver you from the counsel of spies.*

RASHI, SHEMOS 13:16

Before the conquest of Eretz Yisrael, the Jews requested to send spies into the land to check out whether it was indeed all that Hashem had promised. Naturally this constituted a grave offense, for it implied a lack of trust in the Almighty. Yehoshua, Moshe *Rabbenu*'s closest disciple, was chosen to be the spy that represented his tribe. Before they left on their mission, Moshe beseeched Hashem to protect Yehoshua from the evil counsel of the other spies and asked for Divine Mercy so that Yehoshua would not become corrupted by their *lashon ha-ra* (evil report).

The reason Moshe prayed for Yehoshua and not the others was that he felt his disciple would be particularly susceptible. Yehoshua knew that it had been Divinely decreed that Moshe would not enter Eretz Yisrael. He knew that by conquering the land, he would no longer have his beloved *rebbe* in this world. Therefore, Moshe was concerned that Yehoshua might bring back a bad report in order to defer the inevitable.

How powerful is the *talmid*'s need to observe and draw encouragement from his *rebbe*.

# *An Image Frozen in Time*

## *Personal Memories of*
### *Maran Ha-gaon Rav Simcha Wasserman ztz"l*

I sat at Reb Simcha's bedside, my hand firmly clasping his. Every few minutes, Reb Simcha would open his eyes and look at me, the faintest glimmer of a smile appearing on his face. I smiled back, but there were tears behind *my* smile. It was difficult to think that there might come a time when I would no longer have the *zechus* to sit beside him and bask in the glow of his holy radiance. So instead, I directed my thoughts to the first time we met.

It was at the home of Dr. and Mrs. Eisner, prominent Torah *askanim* from Flatbush, and I was delivering a *shiur* to a large group who was gathered there. When I was through speaking, Dr. Eisner came over to where I was talking with some people and whispered to me that if I would like to meet the *rosh yeshivah*, Reb Simcha Wasserman, who was staying in their home, he would be happy to introduce me.

I had only known Reb Simcha until then by his reputa-

169

tion as an extraordinary scholar whose Torah erudition had become nothing less than legendary. Of course, I was eager to meet him, and thrilled at the prospect of having the opportunity to converse with such a *gadol.* I did not realize, however, as I walked towards the Eisners' kitchen, how profound and enduring an effect this meeting would have on me.

I retain my first glimpse of Reb Simcha as a precious image frozen in time. He was seated at the kitchen table, a large volume of Talmud opened before him, his forehead furrowed in concentration. Reb Simcha looked up from the *Gemara* as we entered and he immediately smiled. The kindness and warmth he exuded immediately drew me to him. Dr. Eisner introduced us and Reb Simcha and I began to talk. We spoke for over an hour, and when I finally got up to go, Reb Simcha also stood and expressed his pleasure at our having met. I walked out of the kitchen that late February evening, and the one thought that sprang to mind was...I have found a *rebbe* who is unique in his generation.

Throughout the years that followed, Reb Simcha and I spoke, usually by telephone, usually separated by thousands of miles. He lived in Eretz Yisrael and I lived in the United States. But always I felt we were distanced only by geography. The connection I felt with him was a deep kinship that exists only between the closest of brothers, the closest of *chaverim,* the closest *rebbe* and *talmid.* There was no topic I felt I could not, and in fact did not, discuss with him. Reb Simcha's intuitiveness and wisdom were always inspirational to me and never failed to recharge my zeal and enthusiasm in whatever project I was involved.

I can never forget the time I was privileged to observe these qualities firsthand, when Reb Simcha honored my family with a visit to our home. I introduced the *rosh yeshivah* to my boys, who were about ten years old at the time. Reb Simcha placed an affectionate hand on each boy's shoulder and asked a question on the *Gemara* they were learning. It was obvious from their panic-stricken look that the question had been a bit beyond their scope. Immediately, noticing their discomfiture, Reb Simcha answered the question, as if he had only been asking it of himself. Then, he explained his answer and added an interesting story. The boys still remember the story.

Although Reb Simcha was always acutely tuned to every human being's sense of self-esteem, he never considered his own *kavod* to be important. While staying in the Eisner home, during the course of Shabbos it was mentioned that my shul's annual *Melaveh Malkah* would take place that *motza'ei Shabbos*. I did not send Reb Simcha an invitation so as not to obligate him. We had just started the program when the door of the hall opened, and without fanfare, in walked Reb Simcha. He wished everyone seated nearby a *gutte voch* and sat down at a table near the door.

I knew Reb Simcha to always be punctilious and stringent with himself when it came to the observance of any *halachah*. We were traveling to Washington together, and as soon as the plane took off, I took out a small *kuntres* (pamphlet) I had bought in New York and began reading it. Reb Simcha looked over my shoulder and asked whether, when I finished reading it, he could borrow it. Without a moment's hesitation, I handed him the small booklet. He refused, "No, no, only when you're finished with it will I take it." No amount of persuasion on my part could change Reb Simcha's mind. He would wait until I finished, he insisted. I quickly went through the *kuntrus* and gave it to him. Reb Simcha became very engrossed in it for a while and then raised his head and said, "This is quite interesting. I would like to buy it." He began reaching into his pocket to pay me. "Reb Simcha, please!" I protested. "It was only a few *perutos*. Please accept it as a gift."

"No," he said kindly, with his gentle smile, "*Sonei matanos yichyeh* — he who hates gifts will live long" (Mishlei

15:27), and he would not settle back to continue reading the booklet until he had paid me the three dollars it had cost.

The breadth of Reb Simcha's Torah knowledge was phenomenal, and to talk in learning with him was a *ben Torah*'s dream fulfilled. Nevertheless, Reb Simcha always strove in his learning to reach even greater heights.

Once, he gave me a rare glimpse into the kind of *chinnuch* he had received from Reb Elchanan *ztz"l*, his father. He also explained how, having such a father and such an upbringing, he could not possibly have regarded the learning of Torah any differently. [The love and veneration Reb Simcha felt for Reb Elchanan, even dozens of years after he had been martyred at the hands of the Nazis, *yimach shemam*, became manifest to me when I had occasion to serve as a witness at a *chupah* along with Reb Simcha. When Reb Simcha signed his name on the document, he very simply signed: Elazar Simcha ben.... He then added approximately two lines of encomiums after his beloved father's name.]

"My father's shoes were no longer wearable," he once recounted to me, "and he asked me to go to the store and buy him a new pair. I ran to do the errand quickly, bought the shoes, came back, and gave them to my father. He put the shoes on and while we were out walking, I noticed that he appeared perturbed.

"When I asked him about it, he answered, 'My son, the laces upset me. I usually don't wear shoes with laces. Now I will have to spend time lacing my shoes, unlacing them when a lace breaks, tying them in the morning, untying them at night; they will require precious time that could be used instead for learning.'"

I remembered this story of Reb Simcha's boyhood as I sat by his side during the last days of his life. I came back to the present with a jolt, when suddenly the door of the hospital room burst open and an Oriental nurse bustled in. In a loud

Maran Ha-gaon Rav Simcha Wasserman *ztz"l*
at an Eisner family *simchah.*

and hearty voice, she called to Reb Simcha, "Rabbi Wasserman! Rabbi Wasserman! How are you doing? Come on now,
you've got to get better. The world needs you! *We* need you,
Rabbi Wasserman." This from a gentile nurse.

Reb Simcha, who barely had any strength left, nevertheless mustered the strength to shrug his shoulders and lift his
eyebrows in reply. He obviously felt it important to politely

173

acknowledge the nurse's good wishes. This was the caliber of gentility and refinement that Reb Simcha possessed. This was the regard that Reb Simcha showed to anyone and everyone.

Indeed, I thought, we need you, Reb Simcha. *Klal Yisrael* as a whole needs you. I and countless others need your inspiring presence.

Today, sadly, we have only the remembrances. Fortunately, we have Torah and *avodah* which we can draw upon whenever we are in need of solace and encouragement. Lately, I have been turning to it more and more. We need you, Reb Simcha — may you be a *melitz yosher* for all your children.

# Glossary

The following glossary provides a partial explanation of some of the Hebrew, Aramaic (A.), and Yiddish (Y.) words and phrases used in this book. The spellings and explanations reflect the way the specific word is used herein. Often, there are alternate spellings and meanings for the words.

**ACHARONIM:** *the Later Authorities, post 16th century scholars.*
**ACHDUS:** *unity.*
**ASKANIM:** *influential members of the community.*
**AVODAH:** *worship.*
**AVOS:** *the Patriarchs.*
**BA'ALEI CHESED:** *compassionate individuals.*
**BALEBASIM:** *(Y.) laymen.*
**BASHERT:** *(Y.) preordained; destined.*
**BEIS HA-KEVAROS:** *the cemetery.*
**BEIS HA-MIKDASH:** *the Holy Temple in Jerusalem.*
**BEIS MIDRASH:** *a "house of study"; the study hall of a yeshiva.*
**BENTCH:** *(Y.) to recite a blessing; to recite the Grace after Meals.*
**BIMAH:** *the dais in the synagogue from which the Torah is read.*
**BIRCHOS HA-SHACHAR:** *the blessings recited in the morning.*
**CHASAN:** *a bridegroom.*
**CHASHUVE TZIBBUR:** *(Y.) an important community or congregation.*
**CHINNUCH:** *Jewish education.*
**CHOZRIM B'TESHUVAH:** *formerly non-observant Jews who return to Jewish practice and observance.*
**DATI:** *religious; a religious person.*
**DERASHAH (-SHOS):** *Torah sermon(s).*
**DIVREI ELOKIM CHAYIM:** *lit., "words of the living God," an expression meaning absolute truth.*

**DOR HA-PELAGAH:** *a generation characterized by conflict and disunity.*
**GABBAI:** *a synagogue official.*
**GADOL:** *a great Torah sage and leader.*
**GALUS:** *the exile.*
**GASHMIYUS:** *corporeality; materialism.*
**GOLDENE MEDINAH:** *(Y.) lit., the "golden country"; the United States.*
**GUTTE VOCH:** *(Y.) "[May you have a] good week."*
**HAFTARAH:** *a chapter from the Prophets read in the synagogue on Shabbos after the weekly portion of the Torah is read.*
**HA-KADOSH BARUCH HU:** *the Holy One, Blessed be He.*
**HA-MOTZI:** *"Who brings forth [bread from the earth]", the blessing recited over bread.*
**HASHGACHAH PRATIS:** *Divine providence.*
**HASHKAFAH:** *religious outlook; philosophy.*
**HILCHOS SHABBOS:** *the laws of Sabbath observance.*
**KADDISH YASOM:** *lit., the "orphan's Kaddish."*
**KALLAH:** *a bride; a daughter-in-law.*
**KAPOTE:** *(Y.) a caftan worn by certain Chasidim.*
**KAVOD:** *honor; dignity.*
**KIBBUD AV V'EM:** *[the mitzvah of] honoring one's mother and father.*
**KLAL YISRAEL:** *the Jewish People.*
**KO'ACH:** *strength.*

175

**KOLLEL:** *a center for advanced Torah study for adult students, mostly married men.*
**KORBANOS:** *sacrifices.*
**LICHT:** *(Y.) light.*
**LICHT BENTCHEN:** *(Y.) candle-lighting.*
**MA'ASIM:** *deeds; occurrences.*
**MABUL:** *a flood; the Flood.*
**MANHIG RUCHANI:** *a spiritual leader.*
**MATANAH:** *a gift.*
**MECHANECH:** *a Torah teacher; an educator.*
**MECHILAH:** *forgiveness.*
**MEFARSHIM:** *commentators.*
**MELAVEH MALKAH:** *a festive meal on Saturday night honoring the departing Sabbath queen.*
**MESIRAS NEFESH:** *self-sacrifice; dedication.*
**MISPALLELIM:** *worshipers; a congregation.*
**MOSER NEFESH:** *a self-sacrificing and dedicated person.*
**MOTZA'EI SHABBOS:** *Saturday night.*
**NICHUM AVEILIM:** *comforting mourners.*
**OLEH REGEL:** *a pilgrim to the Holy Temple.*
**PASUK:** *a Torah verse.*
**PERUTOS:** *coins of small denomination.*
**POKE'ACH IVRIM:** *"Who gives sight to the blind," one of the morning blessings.*
**POSHUTE YID:** *(Y.) a simple Jew.*
**RIBBONO SHEL OLAM:** *Master of the Universe.*
**RISHONIM:** *the Early Authorities, scholars of the 11th – 16th century.*

**RUACH:** *spirit; enthusiasm.*
**SANDAK:** *the person who has the honor of holding the baby at a bris.*
**SEUDAH SHELISHIS:** *the third Shabbos meal.*
**SHA'ATNEZ:** *a garment which contains a mixture of wool and linen, the wearing of which is prohibited by the Torah.*
**SHALACH MANOS:** *(Y.) gift packages of food sent on Purim.*
**SHALIACH:** *an emissary; a messenger.*
**SHALOM ZACHAR:** *a Friday night party honoring a newborn son.*
**SHE'ELOS:** *halachic questions.*
**SHLISSEL:** *(Y.) a key.*
**SHOCHET:** *a ritual slaughterer.*
**SHOMER TORAH U-MITZVOS:** *a religious Jew.*
**SIYATTA DI-SHMAYA:** *(A.) Divine assistance.*
**TALMID CHACHAM:** *a Torah scholar.*
**TECHUM SHABBOS:** *the Sabbath boundary.*
**TEFILLAH (-LOS):** *prayer(s).*
**YAMIM NORAIM:** *the Days of Awe — Rosh Hashanah and Yom Kippur.*
**YASHER KO'ACH:** *(colloq.) "Congratulations!" "Good for you!"*
**YIMACH SHEMAM:** *"May their names be blotted out."*
**YIREI SHAMAYIM:** *God-fearing; one who is a God-fearing Jew.*
**ZECHUS:** *merit; privilege.*
**ZIVUG:** *(Y.) a predestined mate.*